THE WITCH'S CHRONICLE

A HISTORY OF WITCHCRAFT

CERRIDWEN MAEVE

CONTENTS

INTRODUCTION

In the small village of Salem, Massachusetts, in 1692, the air was thick with suspicion. The townspeople gathered in hushed circles, their whispers weaving tales of witchcraft and dark arts. It was a time when the mere accusation of witchcraft could send a shiver down the spine, leading to a trial where community, fear, and superstition collided. This was not an isolated incident but part of a larger tapestry of witch hunts that spanned continents and centuries, leaving an indelible mark on history.

This book sets out to explore the intricate and multifaceted history of witchcraft. It aims to unravel the cultural, societal, and historical impacts of witchcraft across various geographies and eras. From the witch trials in Europe to the rituals in African tribes, witchcraft has been a potent force in shaping societies. This book seeks to illuminate these stories and provide a deeper understanding of their significance.

Our journey begins with an overview of key themes and topics. We will traverse the globe, exploring lesser-known events and practices, and examining how witchcraft intersects with issues of gender, power, and societal norms. This global perspective will help us appreciate the complexity and diversity of witchcraft beliefs and practices.

Why, then, does the history of witchcraft still matter today? In many ways, witchcraft has influenced modern cultural identities and feminist movements. It continues to shape societal stereotypes and remains a symbol of both fear and empowerment. Understanding its history allows us to better comprehend its role in contemporary society.

My personal motivation for writing this book stems from a passion for dispelling myths and stereotypes about witchcraft. I aim to promote a deeper understanding of its historical and cultural significance. Witchcraft is often misunderstood, and I believe that by examining its roots, we can challenge preconceived notions and foster a more nuanced view.

Throughout the book, we will explore several key themes and questions. How have perceptions of witchcraft changed over time? What impact have these perceptions had on societal structures? These questions will guide our narrative as we seek answers and insights.

Readers can expect to gain a comprehensive understanding of the complex legacy of witchcraft. This book offers educational insights and engaging narratives that reveal the enduring impact of witchcraft on modern society. By examining historical events and cultural practices, we can better understand the forces that have shaped our world.

I invite you to join me on this journey through history. Together, we will uncover the stories and events that have defined witchcraft across the ages. This exploration will challenge preconceived notions and provide a fresh perspective on a topic that continues to fascinate and intrigue.

Let us embark on this journey through the centuries, exploring the shadows and uncovering the truths that lie within the history of witchcraft. The path is winding, the stories are many, and the lessons are profound. Welcome to "The Witch's Chronicle: A History of Witchcraft."

CHAPTER 1

ORIGINS OF
WITCHCRAFT BELIEFS

I n the cradle of civilization, where the Tigris and Euphrates rivers curve around the fertile lands of Mesopotamia, whispers of magic and sorcery were not just tales told by the firelight but integral parts of daily life. The ancient Sumerians, who lived over 4,000 years ago, believed in a world where gods walked alongside men and magic could turn the tides of fate. This belief was not just idle fantasy but a structured part of their understanding of the universe. The ašipu, or exorcists, played a pivotal role in this society. They were esteemed as both healers and diviners, bridging the gap between the mundane and the divine. But how did magic shape these ancient societies, and what can we learn from them today?

ANCIENT SORCERY: WITCHCRAFT IN MESOPOTAMIA AND EGYPT

In Mesopotamia, magic and religion were deeply inter-twined. The Enuma Elish, an ancient creation myth, paints a vivid picture of gods shaping the cosmos through divine power. This narrative wasn't just a story; it was a reflection of how the Mesopotamians viewed the world—one where magic and divine intervention were everyday occurrences. The ašipu, or magic practitioners, were central figures in this worldview. They were not merely healers but also scholars, using their knowledge to interpret omens and diagnose ailments. Ašipu directed medical treatments, predicted futures, and performed rituals to ward off evil spirits. They believed that illnesses were often the work of malevolent forces sent by displeased gods. By identifying these forces, the ašipu could restore health and harmony.

Amulets and incantations were tools of the trade for these practitioners, serving both protective and aggressive roles. In daily life, Mesopotamians wore amulets to shield themselves from harm and recited incantations for protection, reflecting their belief in magic's power to influence the gods and alter fate. However, this power was a double-edged sword. While many saw magic as a source of protection, others viewed it with suspicion, fearing its potential for harm. Legal texts from the period reflect this duality, with severe punishments for those found guilty of using sorcery for malevolent purposes.

Archaeological evidence sheds light on these practices.

Excavations of ziggurats—massive temple complexes—reveal artifacts that depict magical rituals and support the historical accounts of Mesopotamian magic. These structures served as both religious and administrative centers, demonstrating how magic was woven into the fabric of governance and societal order. The artifacts found within, such as clay tablets inscribed with spells and rituals, provide tangible proof of the ancient belief in the power of magic.

Turning to Egypt, magic was no less significant. It was considered an essential part of maintaining ma'at, the cosmic order. Egyptian society viewed magic as a divine gift, with priests serving as its most prominent practitioners. The Book of the Dead, a collection of spells designed to guide the deceased through the afterlife, illustrates the Egyptians' reliance on magic to ensure a safe passage into the next world. These spells, meticulously recorded on papyrus, were believed to protect the soul against dangers in the afterlife, reflecting the Egyptians' profound belief in magic's protective powers.

Priests, especially those known as "heka" priests, were at the forefront of magical practices. They mediated between the gods and the people, using their knowledge to perform rituals that ensured the well-being of the state and its citizens. Pharaohs themselves were seen as high priests, wielding magic to sustain their rule and the prosperity of their land. Magic was not limited to the elite; it permeated all levels of society. Women, too, were recognized for their magical abilities, often serving as midwives or healers who employed spells and potions.

The practical applications of magic in Egypt were vast. Healing spells and potions were common, addressing ailments and ensuring health. Amulets, often placed with the dead, were believed to protect and guide souls in the afterlife. Yet, like in Mesopotamia, magic's dual nature was evident. While revered for its protective qualities, it was also feared for its potential to harm, with stories of curses and divine intervention illustrating the fine line between benevolent and malevolent magic.

The cultural intersections between Mesopotamia and Egypt are fascinating. Trade routes facilitated the exchange of ideas and beliefs, leading to shared motifs in their mythologies and deities. This exchange highlights the fluid nature of magical beliefs, evolving and adapting as they spread across cultures. Political structures in both regions also played a role in shaping these practices. The concept of divine kingship, where rulers were seen as earthly representatives of the gods, underscored the importance of magic in maintaining power and control. Legal codes often referenced magic, reflecting its integral role in governance and societal regulation.

MYSTICAL PRACTICES OF THE CELTS AND DRUIDS

In the verdant landscapes of ancient Celtic territories, where the land itself seemed to hum with a mystical energy, the Celts lived in profound connection with nature.

Their spiritual beliefs were deeply woven into the natural world, with sacred groves and natural sites serving as the heart of their religious practices. These groves, often composed of oak, yew, and ash trees, were not just mere clusters of trees but sacred spaces where the divine was palpable. Here, under the rustling leaves and shifting shadows, the druids—Celtic priests and wise ones—performed rituals and communed with the spirits. These sacred spaces were the epicenters of Celtic spirituality, places where the boundaries between the earthly and the spiritual blurred.

The Celts were an oral society, their knowledge and traditions passed down through generations by word of mouth. This oral tradition was vital, as it preserved the collective memory and wisdom of the people. The druids, as custodians of this knowledge, held immense power and influence. They were more than religious leaders; they were the keepers of the law, the healers, and the advisors to chieftains. Their counsel was sought in matters of both war and peace, and their judgment was respected in disputes. Druidic influence extended into the political realm, where they acted as mediators and diplomats, shaping the fate of tribes through their guidance.

Druidic ceremonies were rich in symbolism and steeped in the cycles of nature. The Celts celebrated seasonal festivals such as Samhain and Beltane, marking the transitions between light and dark, life and death. Samhain, a festival heralding the darker half of the year, was a time when the veil between the worlds was thin, and spirits roamed the earth. Fires blazed in the night as offerings were made to ancestors and protective rituals were performed to guard against malevolent forces. Beltane, on the other hand, celebrated the return of life and light, with bonfires, dancing, and rituals to ensure fertility and prosperity. These festivals, alongside rites of passage and community gatherings, reinforced social bonds and connected the Celts to the rhythm of the earth.

However, the arrival of the Romans marked a turning point in Celtic magical practices. Roman accounts, such as those from Julius Caesar, often depicted druids as both wise sages and formidable opponents, reflecting the complex relationship between the two cultures. As the Romans expanded their empire, they sought to suppress and assimilate the cultures they encountered. Celtic rituals and druidic teachings were seen as threats to Roman rule and were systematically targeted for elimination. Yet, despite this suppression, many Celtic rituals survived, often merging with Roman practices. The resilience of the druids and their traditions is a testament to the enduring power of their beliefs, as they adapted and persisted in the face of conquest.

The legacy of the Celts and their druids continues to captivate our imagination today. Their deep connection to nature and the spiritual realm resonates with those who seek meaning beyond the material world. The sacred groves, the oral traditions, and the rituals that once defined Celtic spirituality now serve as reminders of a time when humanity lived in harmony with the natural world. The resilience of the druids and the survival of their traditions amidst the Roman conquest highlight the enduring power of cultural identity and the capacity of human belief to adapt and thrive, even under the most challenging circumstances. The echoes of Celtic spirituality remind us that the world is full of mysteries waiting to be uncovered, urging us to look beyond the surface and embrace the unknown.

CHAPTER 2
WITCHCRAFT IN CLASSICAL ANTIQUITY

I n the dim glow of ancient Greece, where philosophy and myth intertwined, the night sky held more than stars—it held secrets. Among these mysteries, one figure emerged as a beacon for those who walked the path of magic and the arcane: Hecate, the goddess who stood at the crossroads of the human and the divine, the known and the unknown.

HECTATE AND THE GREEK WITCH TRADITIONS

She is a figure both feared and revered, her presence felt wherever the boundaries of reality blurred. Hecate, known as the goddess of witchcraft, magic, and the night, held sway over heaven, earth, and sea, a testament to her formidable power. Born of the Titans Perses and Asteria, she inherited a legacy that touched the mortal and the divine. In Hesiod's "Theogony," she is depicted as a singular force, a guardian of the marginalized and a guide in the shadowed realms. Her association with crossroads—literal and metaphorical—symbolized her role as a guide and protector, where offerings were made to seek her favor and guidance. Her image often adorned Greek vase paintings, depicting her with twin torches, illuminating the dark paths of the unknown.

The Greek world was rich with magical practices, embedded deeply within its social fabric. Love potions and curse tablets, known as katadesmoi, were tools of influence and desire. These tablets were inscribed with curses intended to bind or harm rivals, often buried in secret places like graves or sanctuaries, where their power could seep into the earth and beyond. Love spells, too, found their place in the hearts and homes of the Greeks, offering the promise of passion or the mending of a broken heart. Magical papyri documented spells for everything from protection to personal gain, reflecting a society where magic was both a personal and public endeavor. These spells were often complex, requiring precise incantations and rituals, and they reveal a culture where the pursuit of control over fate was a common thread.

In Greek literature, witches occupied a space both fascinating and fearsome. Characters like Circe and Medea stand as enduring symbols of this duality. Circe, in "The Odyssey," embodies the enchantress who transforms men into beasts, wielding her power with both benevolence and menace. Her island, Aeaea, is a realm of transformation and magic, where the lines between reality and illusion blur.

Medea, in contrast, is a figure of tragic complexity in Euripides' play. Her story is one of love, betrayal, and vengeance, with her magical prowess used to both heal and harm. The Thessalian witches, renowned for their skill in the dark arts, added to the lore of fear and fascination, their reputation casting a long shadow over the Greek imagination. These narratives, rich with symbolism, reflect a culture that grappled with the power of the unknown and the moral ambiguities it entailed.

Magic was a part of daily life in Greece, woven into the very fabric of society. Love spells and potions were not merely the stuff of legends but tools used in everyday interactions, from courtship to conflict resolution. Public attitudes towards magic were complex, with female practitioners often viewed with suspicion and awe. Women who practiced magic could be seen as healers, offering remedies and comfort, or as threats, wielding powers that defied societal norms. This dual perception of women in magic highlights the tensions between empowerment and fear that permeated Greek culture.

Philosophy and religion in Greece provided frameworks to understand and interpret these magical practices. Plato, whose ideas continue to influence Western thought, viewed magic with skepticism, associating it with the manipulation of the soul. He believed that true wisdom lay in the pursuit of knowledge and virtue, not in the enchantments of the sorcerer. The Eleusinian Mysteries, secretive religious rites held in honor of Demeter and Persephone, offered mystical experiences that blurred the lines between life and death, the mortal and the divine. These mysteries, shrouded in secrecy, provided a space where the mystical aspects of the human experience could be explored and celebrated.

Archaeological discoveries provide tangible links to these ancient practices, offering glimpses into the world of Greek magic. Curse tablets, or defixiones, inscribed with invocations and buried in secret places, reveal the personal and societal conflicts that drove individuals to seek supernatural intervention. These tablets often contained elaborate curses, calling upon deities and spirits to enact vengeance or justice. Magical papyri, with their detailed spells and rituals, offer further insights into the practical applications of Greek magic, from healing to protection. These artifacts serve as a testament to a world where the boundaries between the seen and unseen were fluid, where magic provided a means to navigate the uncertainties of life.

As you explore these ancient practices, consider the ways in which they resonate with contemporary beliefs and rituals. How do these stories of magic and mystery reflect our own desires and fears? What can they teach us about the enduring human quest for control and understanding? The world of Greek witchcraft, with its rich tapestry of myth and magic, offers a window into a world where the divine and the human intersected, where the night held secrets waiting to be discovered.

SORCERY IN THE ROMAN EMPIRE: FROM MAGIC TO HERESY

In the heart of the Roman Empire, where the echoes of grandeur and conquest were ever-present, magic flourished in the shadows of daily life, serving both mundane needs and deeper, more enigmatic purposes. Roman society, with its intricate blend of practicality and superstition, embraced a variety of magical practices that were as widespread as they were diverse. Among these, the defixiones, or curse tablets, stand out as both tools of personal vendettas and reflections of societal tensions. These inscribed pieces of lead or pottery were often hidden in graves or thrown into wells, intended to invoke the gods' wrath upon enemies or rivals. These tablets, etched with invocations and curses, provide a fascinating glimpse into the personal conflicts and desires that drove individuals to seek supernatural intervention. The presence of defixiones in legal disputes underscores their significance, revealing a society where the lines between law and magic were often blurred.

The haruspex, a type of diviner, played a crucial role in Roman public and private life, wielding the power to interpret the will of the gods through the examination of animal entrails. These diviners were called upon to guide decisions ranging from state affairs to personal matters, their interpretations believed to reveal the future and the gods' favor or displeasure. Their presence at public ceremonies and private consultations highlights the deep-rooted belief in the power of divination to influence the course of events. Haruspicy was not merely a superstition but an institutionalized practice, integral to the Roman understanding of fate and fortune.

Legal and social attitudes towards magic in Rome were complex, marked by both reverence and suspicion. The Lex Cornelia de sicariis et veneficiis, a law enacted under the dictator Sulla, specifically targeted poisoners and practitioners of harmful magic, reflecting the state's desire to curb the perceived threats of sorcery. This law illustrates the Roman approach to magic as a potentially dangerous force, one that needed regulation and control. Public trials of accused sorcerers were not uncommon, with punishments ranging from exile to execution, depending on the nature and severity of the alleged crimes. These trials served as public spectacles, reinforcing societal norms and the boundaries of acceptable behavior.

Roman literature offers a rich tapestry of narratives that depict witches and magic, each story adding layers to the cultural understanding of sorcery. Horace's portrayal of Canidia, a witch who embodies malevolence and dark power, reflects the fear and fascination that surrounded magical practitioners. In Seneca's "Medea," the main character uses her knowledge of magic to exact revenge, her actions driven by intense emotion and moral ambiguity. Pliny the Elder's accounts provide a more pragmatic view, documenting various magical practices with a blend of skepticism and curiosity. These literary works not only entertained but also shaped public perceptions, embedding magic deeply within the cultural consciousness.

The Roman Empire, with its expansive reach, was a melting pot of cultures and beliefs, and magic was no exception. The influence of Egyptian magic, known for its complex rituals and rich symbology, permeated Roman society, leading to a blending of local and imported magical traditions. Egyptian practices, such as the use of amulets and spells, were adapted and integrated into Roman rituals, illustrating the dynamic interchange of ideas. This cultural exchange enriched the Roman magical landscape, creating a tapestry of practices that were both diverse and inter-connected.

Religion in Rome was a tapestry woven with traditional beliefs and emerging monotheistic ideas, creating a back-drop of tension and transformation. As Christianity began to take root, perceptions of magic shifted, with sorcery increasingly associated with heresy and paganism. This shift marked a turning point in the history of witchcraft, as the burgeoning Christian doctrine positioned itself against practices it deemed contrary to its teachings. The blending of traditional Roman and newly introduced religious prac-tices played a crucial role in this transition, as they coex-isted and sometimes clashed, impacting the development and perception of magic.

Notable figures of the Roman era, accused or celebrated for their magical abilities, further illustrate the complex relationship between magic and society. Apuleius, a philosopher and author, famously defended himself against charges of using magic to win the affections of a wealthy widow in his "Apologia," a defense that remains a rich source of insight into Roman legal and cultural norms. His trial underscores the precarious position of those associated with magic, where intellectual pursuits and supernatural practices often intersected. Emperors, too, were not immune to the allure of magic. Nero, known for his eccentricities and tyrannical rule, was rumored to have dabbled in the occult, his reign marked by a fascination with the mystical and the forbidden.

In the Roman Empire, magic was a powerful undercurrent, shaping the lives of individuals and the trajectory of the empire itself. This chapter's exploration of magic's evolution, societal roles, and cultural exchanges sets the stage for understanding how these ancient practices have influenced modern perceptions and beliefs. As we transition to the next chapter, the legacy of Roman magic echoes through time, inviting us to consider the enduring impact of these practices on the world today.

CHAPTER 3
WITCHCRAFT AND EARLY CHRISTIANITY

PAGAN RITUALS AND THE CHRISTIANIZATION OF EUROPE

In the twilight of the Roman Empire, as the flicker of pagan temples began to dim, a new faith emerged, weaving its way across Europe with a promise of salvation and eternal life. This was a time of profound transformation, where the familiar rituals of old gods met the burgeoning power of Christianity. The clash between these two worlds was not one of immediate conquest but a gradual blending, where old and new beliefs danced in a complex tapestry of faith. As Christianity spread, its early missionaries embarked on a daunting mission to convert pagan Europe, navigating a landscape deeply rooted in ancient customs and rituals. These early Christians, armed with the message of Christ, faced communities where pagan traditions were more than mere beliefs—they were the very fabric of life, ingrained in the rhythms of nature and the cycles of the seasons.

The conversion efforts were far from straightforward. Rather than eradicating pagan practices, early missionaries often sought to adapt them, creating an amalgamation that allowed for a smoother transition. Pagan festivals, with their rich symbolism and communal spirit, were recast into Christian holidays. The winter solstice celebration of Yule, with its focus on light returning to the world, was transformed into Christmas, celebrating the birth of Christ as the light of humanity. Similarly, the spring festival of Ostara, a time of renewal and fertility, found new life in Easter, marking the resurrection of Jesus. This adaptation was a strategic move, allowing the old and new to coexist, softening resistance and making Christianity more palatable to those steeped in pagan lore.

The merging of beliefs and practices was not limited to festivals, as elements of paganism found their way into Christian rituals. The veneration of saints, for instance, mirrored the reverence pagans had for their gods and heroes. Many saints took on attributes of local deities, offering protection and performing miracles, thus bridging the gap between the old faith and the new. Christian reinterpretation of pagan symbols also played a crucial role. The cross, a symbol of salvation, found its place alongside ancient motifs, creating a visual language that spoke to both pagan and Christian. These practices allowed for a blending of traditions, where the sacred could be found in both the familiar and the unfamiliar.

Yet, not all were willing to abandon their ancestral beliefs so readily. Resistance to Christianization was fierce in certain areas, particularly in rural communities where pagan rituals persisted with vigor. These regions, often isolated and bound by tradition, became strongholds of the old ways. Historical accounts tell of uprisings and defiance, where pagans fought to preserve their cultural identity against the encroaching tide of Christianity. These acts of resistance were seen as both heroic and heretical, challenging the authority of a Church determined to unify belief under its doctrine.

The persistence of pagan customs was evident in various practices, from funeral rites to seasonal celebrations. These rites, deeply embedded in the cultural psyche, were hard to erase. The Church, recognizing the impossibility of outright eradication, often sought to moderate and incorporate them. For instance, the ritual lament, a significant aspect of pagan funerals, was initially condemned by Christian authorities but eventually absorbed into Christian ceremonies with added theological explanations. This pragmatic approach allowed the Church to maintain control while respecting the cultural heritage of the people.

As paganism and Christianity intertwined, perceptions of witchcraft underwent a significant transformation. Pagan deities, once revered and worshipped, were increasingly demonized. The Church labeled them as evil spirits, casting them as adversaries in a cosmic battle between good and evil. This shift in perception was pivotal in shaping early Christian views on witchcraft. Witches, who were often seen as practitioners of ancient rites and keepers of forbidden knowledge, became targets of suspicion and fear. They were portrayed as those who consorted with the devil, wielding powers that threatened the Christian order.

The portrayal of witches as adherents of forbidden pagan rites was not merely a theological stance but a reflection of broader societal anxieties. In a rapidly changing world, where the old and new were in constant flux, the figure of the witch became a symbol of resistance to the growing dominance of Christianity. This demonization served to reinforce the authority of the Church, drawing clear lines between the sacred and the profane, the acceptable and the forbidden.

As you turn the pages of this chapter, consider the echoes of this past in the modern world. The interplay between pagan and Christian beliefs laid the groundwork for the complex perceptions of witchcraft that persist to this day. It is a history that speaks to the resilience of cultural identity and the enduring power of belief.

THE ROLE OF HERESY IN WITCHCRAFT ACCUSATIONS

In the early days of Christianity, as the fledgling Church sought to define its beliefs, the concept of heresy emerged as a powerful tool for enforcing orthodoxy. Heresy, fundamentally, referred to beliefs or practices that deviated from the established doctrine of the Church. It was not just a theological disagreement; it was seen as a threat to the unity and purity of the Christian faith. As the Church Fathers grappled with defining the core tenets of Christianity, theological debates raged, often giving rise to heretical movements. Among these, Gnosticism stood out, offering a mystical interpretation of Christianity that emphasized secret knowledge and spiritual enlightenment. Gnostics viewed the material world as inherently flawed, created by a lesser deity, and believed that only through hidden wisdom could one achieve salvation. This belief system, with its esoteric teachings, posed a direct challenge to the Church's authority and its emphasis on a more accessible, communal path to salvation.

The connection between heresy and witchcraft became increasingly pronounced as the Church worked to solidify its doctrinal boundaries. Heretical beliefs, with their emphasis on mystical knowledge and alternative spiritual practices, often intersected with the realm of what we now consider witchcraft. The suspicion that heretics engaged in magical practices was not unfounded. Many heretical sects incorporated elements of mysticism and ritual that the orthodox Church viewed with deep suspicion. This association was further fueled by the Church's portrayal of heretics as conduits of malevolent forces seeking to undermine Christian teachings. The fear of the unknown, compounded by the Church's warnings, led to a climate where accusations of witchcraft became a convenient means of silencing dissent and reinforcing doctrine.

The Church's stance on heresy and its association with witchcraft was formalized through a series of councils and edicts. The Council of Elvira, convened in the early fourth century, issued decrees that condemned practices seen as incompatible with Christian teachings. This council set a precedent for how the Church would handle deviations from its dogma. Similarly, the Synod of Laodicea played a crucial role in shaping the Church's approach to magical practices. Its canons explicitly prohibited the use of enchantments and spells, equating them with pagan and heretical practices. These decrees reinforced the Church's authority and laid the groundwork for the systematic persecution of those deemed heretical or engaged in witchcraft.

Throughout history, notable heresy trials have highlighted the complex relationship between heretical beliefs and accusations of witchcraft. One of the earliest and most significant cases was that of Priscillian of Ávila, a bishop in fourth-century Spain. Priscillian's ascetic lifestyle and teachings, which included elements of mysticism, attracted a following that alarmed the established Church. Accused of heresy and sorcery, Priscillian was ultimately executed, marking a pivotal moment in the history of Christian heresy trials. His case set a precedent for the involvement of secular authorities in religious matters and highlighted the Church's willingness to conflate heresy with witchcraft to maintain control.

Another significant example is the Cathars, a Christian dualist movement that flourished in southern France during the 12th and 13th centuries. The Cathars, with their belief in two opposing forces of good and evil, challenged the Church's teachings on the nature of God and the material world. Their practices, which included secret rituals and a rejection of traditional Church sacraments, were deemed heretical. The Church launched a crusade against the Cathars, culminating in the Albigensian Crusade, a brutal campaign that sought to eradicate the movement. Accusations of witchcraft were leveled against the Cathars, further demonizing them in the eyes of orthodox Christians and justifying the extreme measures taken against them.

The intertwining of heresy and witchcraft in these cases underscores the Church's broader strategy of using accusations of sorcery as a tool for maintaining doctrinal purity and societal control. By framing heretical beliefs as not only spiritually dangerous but also as conduits of dark and malevolent forces, the Church reinforced its moral and spiritual authority. This legacy of fear and persecution would echo through the centuries, influencing later witch hunts and shaping the cultural perceptions of witchcraft as fundamentally opposed to the orthodox Christian worldview.

As we close this chapter, consider the weight of these historical narratives and their enduring impact. The Church's efforts to define its doctrine and suppress dissent created a climate where fear and suspicion flourished, laying the groundwork for future persecutions. This intersection of heresy and witchcraft reveals the complexities of faith, power, and control in shaping religious history.

~

CHAPTER 4
THE MEDIEVAL WITCH HUNTS

T he chill of a medieval courtroom can be felt through the pages of history, where the accused stood trembling before the bench, their fate hanging in the balance.

THE MALLEUS MALEFICARUM AND ITS INFLUENCE

In a time when fear and superstition ruled, the mere whisper of witchcraft could spark a trial that might end with a pyre's blaze. At the heart of this hysteria was a book that would become infamous: the *Malleus Maleficarum*, or the Hammer of Witches. Written in 1487 by Heinrich Kramer, a clergyman with a fervent zeal, and Jacob Sprenger, a theologian whose involvement remains debated, this text was intended to be a definitive guide in identifying, prosecuting, and eradicating witches. Kramer's obsession with rooting out witches was fueled by his own experiences and frustrations with ecclesiastical authorities who were often skeptical of witchcraft's prevalence. The Church, grappling with its own internal struggles, eventually gave the book the papal endorsement it needed to gain traction, though it was not an official decree. This endorsement, however, lent the text a veneer of authority that transcended its origins, embedding it deeply in the consciousness of medieval Europe.

The *Malleus Maleficarum* stands as a chilling testament to the era's beliefs and fears. Its pages meticulously outline the criteria for identifying witches, a process steeped in paranoia and superstition. The book described witches as primarily women, asserting that their supposed weaker nature made them more susceptible to the devil's temptations. It perpetuated the stereotype of witches as diabolical agents, engaging in acts that ranged from the absurd to the horrific. The authors provided a disturbing methodology for interrogation and prosecution, advocating for the use of torture to extract confessions. This approach not only legitimized but encouraged the most brutal forms of questioning, setting a precedent for witch trials that would follow. The structure of the text, divided into three parts, systematically guided inquisitors through the identification, trial, and punishment of witches, leaving little room for doubt or mercy.

The influence of the *Malleus Maleficarum* on the spread of witch hunts across Europe cannot be overstated. As the printing press disseminated its pages far and wide, the book's reach extended beyond borders and language barriers, finding its way into the hands of inquisitors and judges from Germany to Scotland. Each new translation and edition was marked by a pernicious increase in witch trials, as towns and villages, caught in the throes of fear, turned to the text for guidance. The *Malleus* became a reference point in countless trials, its authority unquestioned by those who wielded it. Case studies from this period reveal the text's profound impact. In Bamberg and Würzburg, large-scale witch hunts saw hundreds executed, their trials echoing the methods and reasoning found within the *Malleus*. These events, though extreme, were not isolated, reflecting a broader pattern of persecution that swept through Europe like a wildfire.

The long-term effects of the *Malleus Maleficarum* on perceptions of witchcraft have left an indelible mark on history. The book's portrayal of witches as insidious threats lurking within the fabric of society fueled enduring stereotypes and fears. Witches, as depicted in the *Malleus*, were not merely practitioners of forbidden arts; they were agents of chaos, accused of inflicting harm on individuals and communities alike. This image persisted long after the witch hunts waned, influencing cultural narratives and popular media for centuries. The text's impact on legal practices was equally significant. It provided a framework that was adopted by both secular and ecclesiastical courts, solidifying the use of inquisitorial procedures and torture in witch trials. The *Malleus* effectively codified the prosecution of witches, embedding its principles in legal systems that would outlast the medieval period.

The societal and cultural reactions to the *Malleus Maleficarum* were complex and far-reaching. Its influence heightened fear and suspicion, particularly in rural communities where belief in witchcraft was already pervasive. The book's emphasis on women as the primary culprits of witchcraft exacerbated existing gender dynamics, leading to a disproportionate targeting of women in witch trials. This gendered persecution reflected broader societal anxieties about women's roles and agency, casting a long shadow over gender relations that would endure for generations. As accusations spread, communities found themselves caught in a web of fear and distrust, where neighbor turned against neighbor and the specter of witchcraft loomed large. The *Malleus Maleficarum*, in its relentless pursuit of witches, laid the groundwork for a legacy of persecution and fear that would echo through the annals of history, shaping the way witchcraft was perceived and prosecuted for centuries to come.

WITCH TRIALS IN THE HOLY ROMAN EMPIRE

During the height of the witch hunts, the Holy Roman Empire was a patchwork of territories, each with its own approach to dealing with the perceived threat of witchcraft. This vast realm, with its myriad duchies, principalities, and bishoprics, became fertile ground for witch trials, particularly in regions like Bavaria and Franconia. These areas, known for their fervent religiosity and complex political structures, saw some of the most intense witch-hunting activities. In Franconia, the town of Würzburg became infamous for its trials in the early 17th century, where dozens were accused and executed in a climate of fear and suspicion. Similarly, Bamberg witnessed its own wave of hysteria, with trials that spread like wildfire across the region. These trials were not mere spontaneous eruptions but were often orchestrated events, reflecting a broader pattern of accusations that transcended local boundaries. Demographic trends reveal that a significant number of those accused were women, though men, particularly those in positions of influence, were not immune to suspicion. These patterns highlight the intersection of gender, power, and fear that fueled the witch hunts.

The Würzburg and Bamberg witch trials are emblematic of the period, showcasing both the legal mechanisms and the societal anxieties that drove these events. In Würzburg, Prince-Bishop Julius Echter von Mespelbrunn played a pivotal role, using the trials as a means to consolidate power and enforce religious conformity. His actions were mirrored in Bamberg by Prince-Bishop Johann Georg Fuchs von Dornheim, whose zeal for purging witchcraft earned him the nickname "Hexenbrenner," or "witch burner." Under their leadership, the trials took on a bureaucratic efficiency, with detailed records kept of accusations, confessions, and executions. These trials were characterized by their brutality, with torture used liberally to extract confessions, often implicating others in a widening net of suspicion. The outcomes were grim, with many victims meeting their end at the stake, their confessions serving as both evidence and spectacle.

Religious and political authorities wielded immense influence over the conduct and outcomes of witch trials in the Holy Roman Empire. The Catholic Church, through local bishops and inquisitors, played a significant role in perpetuating the fear of witchcraft, viewing it as a threat to the spiritual order. Protestant leaders, too, were not immune to the allure of witch hunts, often using them to assert their own religious and moral authority. These leaders capitalized on the trials to reinforce their power, presenting themselves as protectors of the faith against a hidden enemy. Political motivations frequently intertwined with religious fervor, as rulers sought to eliminate dissent and consolidate control over their territories. The witch trials offered a convenient tool to suppress opposition, both real and imagined, under the guise of protecting the community from malevolent forces.

The legacy of the witch trials in the Holy Roman Empire is complex, leaving a lasting imprint on historical memory and societal attitudes. By the late 17th century, a gradual decline in trials began to take hold, driven by shifts in judicial practices and a growing skepticism of witchcraft accusations. The brutality and excesses of earlier trials, particularly the rampant use of torture, came under scrutiny, leading to reforms that prioritized evidence and due process. This shift marked a turning point, as the legal system moved away from the extreme measures that had characterized the height of the witch hunts. Public perception, too, began to change, with a growing recognition of the injustices suffered by countless victims. Commemorations and reflections on the witch trials have become a part of modern discourse, serving as a reminder of the dangers of unchecked fear and the abuse of power. These reflections often focus on the lessons learned from history, emphasizing the importance of reason and compassion in the face of societal panic.

As the witch hunts faded into the annals of history, their echoes continued to resonate, shaping cultural narratives and influencing modern interpretations of justice and power. The Holy Roman Empire, with its tapestry of trials and tribulations, offers a poignant example of how fear can be weaponized to control and divide. This chapter, in examining the intricacies of the witch trials within the empire, provides insight into the broader dynamics at play during this tumultuous period. As we move forward, the stories of those who lived and died in the shadow of suspicion remind us of the enduring struggle between fear and understanding, a theme that will continue to unfold in the chapters ahead.

CHAPTER 5

GENDER AND WITCHCRAFT ACCUSATIONS

I magine a village on the cusp of dawn, where a woman's whispered name crackles through the chill air like a threat. In that moment, she is no longer a neighbor, midwife, or friend but a witch—a figure cloaked in shadows and suspicion. This transformation is swift and terrifying, rooted in centuries of cultural narratives that cast women as the embodiment of danger and deceit. Across folklore and fairy tales, the image of the witch emerges as an evil crone, a figure who wields her power with malevolence. These tales, passed down through generations, paint witches as women who defy societal norms, their very existence a challenge to the status quo.

THE WITCH AS A MISOGYNISTIC STEREOTYPE

The stereotype of the female witch draws heavily on the association of female sexuality with witchcraft. In cultures where a woman's virtue was tightly controlled, any deviation from this norm could be seen as a threat. The allure and mystery of female sexuality, often misunderstood and feared, became intertwined with notions of witchcraft. This connection was further reinforced by church teachings that emphasized women's susceptibility to sin. The biblical story of Eve, who succumbed to temptation and led Adam astray, was a powerful narrative used to illustrate women's inherent moral weakness. This portrayal not only justified the control of women's bodies and actions but also fueled the idea that they were more likely to consort with dark forces, their sexuality a tool of the devil.

Misogyny played a central role in the identification and prosecution of witches, with societal attitudes reflecting deep-seated fears of female power. The Malleus Maleficarum, a text infamous for its misogynistic views, outlined the reasons for women's susceptibility to witchcraft. Written in the late 15th century, it became a cornerstone for witch hunts, its pages filled with claims that women were more likely to fall under the devil's influence due to their perceived weaknesses. This text, widely accepted across Europe, provided a blueprint for the persecution of women, framing them as dangerous and deceitful. Midwives and herbalists, women whose roles were vital to their communities, found themselves demonized. Their knowledge of healing and herbs, once seen as gifts, became suspect. The church, wary of any power outside its control, targeted these women, accusing them of using their skills for malevolent purposes.

Art and literature further entrenched the image of women as witches, their portrayals reinforcing societal fears. Francisco Goya's "The Witches' Sabbath" presents a haunting vision of witchcraft, using witches as metaphors to critique societal norms. Goya's work, filled with dark and fantastical imagery, reflects the anxieties of his time, portraying witches as figures of chaos and disruption. Plays and pamphlets from the period also contributed to this narrative, depicting witches as embodiments of evil and disorder. These portrayals, consumed by a public eager for entertainment and scandal, shaped perceptions of women, linking them to witchcraft in the collective imagination.

The intersection of gender and fear is evident in the accusations leveled against women who defied traditional roles. In societies where male authority was paramount, women who challenged these norms were often seen as threats. Whether through independence, knowledge, or defiance, these women became targets, their actions interpreted as signs of witchcraft. Accusations frequently arose from societal anxieties regarding fertility and lineage. In a world where family lines and inheritance were crucial, any deviation from expected roles could stir fear and suspicion. Women who did not marry or bear children, who lived on the fringes of society, often found themselves accused of witchcraft, their independence viewed as unnatural or dangerous.

WOMEN, POWER, AND PERSECUTION

Throughout history, women have occupied roles that, paradoxically, both empowered and endangered them. Within many communities, healers and wise women were revered for their knowledge of herbs and remedies. These women provided essential services in a time when professional medical care was scarce. As community leaders, they wielded a form of power that was both respected and feared. This respect could quickly turn to suspicion, especially when their influence challenged the existing social order. Women who owned property or held sway over local affairs often found themselves targets of jealousy and resentment. Their autonomy was seen as a threat, particularly in patriarchal societies where male authority was the norm. This fear of female independence contributed to accusations of witchcraft, as powerful women were often portrayed as using supernatural means to maintain their status.

Economic and social factors played a significant role in the vulnerability of women to these accusations. Widows, for instance, were particularly at risk. Without the protection of a husband, widows often faced economic insecurity and societal pressure. Their status made them easy targets for accusations, especially if they were perceived to have benefited financially from a husband's death. Rivalries within communities also contributed to the spread of accusations. Disputes over land, resources, or personal grievances could quickly escalate, with witchcraft serving as a convenient weapon to eliminate rivals. Women who were seen as outsiders, perhaps because they did not conform to societal norms, were especially vulnerable. The combination of economic dependency and social isolation created a fertile ground for suspicion and blame.

Historical records are replete with case studies of women who faced accusations of witchcraft, their stories offering a glimpse into the societal dynamics of their time. Anne Boleyn, the much-maligned queen of England, is often mistakenly associated with witchcraft due to the political machinations of her era. While she was executed for treason and adultery, the whispers of witchcraft lingered, fueled by her enemies who sought to tarnish her legacy. Anne's downfall was as much about power and politics as it was about personal vendettas, illustrating how accusations could be wielded to destroy those who threatened the status quo. In contrast, Alice Kyteler, a wealthy woman in 14th-century Ireland, faced direct accusations of witchcraft. Her case highlights the intersection of wealth, influence, and gender. As a successful businesswoman, Alice amassed significant wealth, which drew envy and suspicion. The charges against her were rooted in local disputes and power struggles, with her wealth and independence marking her as an outsider.

The long-term impact of these witch trials on gender relations is profound, reinforcing societal norms that have persisted for centuries. The legacy of witch hunts is evident in the gender stereotypes that continue to influence perceptions of women today. The idea that women who possess power or deviate from traditional roles are dangerous or untrustworthy has deep historical roots. These stereotypes have been challenged by feminist movements, which seek to reclaim and reinterpret the narratives of accused witches. By examining the cultural memory of these witch trials, we gain insight into the ways in which gender hierarchies have been constructed and maintained. Feminist scholars have highlighted how the persecution of witches serves as a metaphor for the broader oppression of women, drawing parallels between past injustices and contemporary struggles for gender equality.

As you reflect on these historical narratives, consider how the stories of persecuted women resonate with modern discussions about power and gender. The trials and tribulations of these women offer lessons about resilience and resistance, challenging us to rethink the ways in which we view power and authority. These narratives remind us that the past is not so distant, and the echoes of history continue to shape our present and future. Understanding the intersections of gender, power, and persecution allows us to better navigate the complexities of our own society, recognizing the enduring impact of these historical injustices. As we move forward, the next chapter will explore how witchcraft's cultural and geographical diversity further enriches our understanding of this multifaceted phenomenon.

CHAPTER 6

WITCHCRAFT ACROSS CULTURES

AFRICAN WITCHCRAFT AND COLONIAL INTERPRETATIONS

I n the heart of African society, where the rhythm of drums echoes through the air and the scent of earth after rain fills the senses, lies a rich tapestry of beliefs and practices surrounding witchcraft. These practices are not mere relics of the past; they are living, breathing elements of culture that shape communities and influence daily life. Across the continent, witchcraft holds diverse meanings and serves various roles, from spiritual guidance to social regulation. At the core of these practices is the concept of "juju," an intricate system of beliefs that encompasses charms, spells, and rituals. Juju acts as a conduit to supernatural energies, offering protection, luck, and success. It can be both benevolent and malevolent, used for healing or harm, reflecting the dual nature of magic itself.

In West African societies, juju plays a crucial role in the spiritual landscape. It is a tool for empowerment and influence, allowing individuals to navigate the complexities of life with divine assistance. Traditional healers, known as "sangomas" in Southern Africa, act as intermediaries between the physical and spiritual worlds. They are revered for their ability to heal, counsel, and guide, drawing on ancestral wisdom and spiritual insight. These practitioners are not merely healers but also custodians of culture, preserving the knowledge passed down through generations. They hold a position of respect and authority, their skills sought in times of illness, conflict, or uncertainty. In many African communities, witchcraft serves as a means of social control and conflict resolution, providing a framework for understanding and addressing community issues.

The diversity of African witchcraft is as vast as the continent itself. In some regions, "witch smellers" are employed to identify individuals practicing harmful magic. These figures wield significant power, their declarations often leading to social ostracism or worse. In West Africa, the practice of "obeah" blends African, European, and indigenous elements, creating a unique spiritual tradition. Obeah is both feared and respected, its practitioners believed to possess the ability to heal or harm with equal ease. Ancestor worship, deeply embedded in many African cultures, intersects with witchcraft, as the spirits of the departed are believed to influence the living world. Ancestors are revered, their guidance sought in matters of family, health, and prosperity.

Witchcraft in Africa is not just a matter of individual belief but a social phenomenon with profound implications. It serves as a lens through which misfortune or illness is explained, providing a narrative for events that defy understanding. When crops fail or sickness strikes, witchcraft offers an explanation, often leading to accusations and retribution. Community councils play a critical role in addressing these accusations, balancing the need for justice with the risk of unrest. These councils mediate conflicts, seeking to restore harmony while maintaining social order. The perception of witchcraft reflects broader societal dynamics, shaping relationships and influencing behavior.

The impact of colonialism on African witchcraft was profound, altering perceptions and practices in ways that continue to resonate. Colonial powers often interpreted African magical practices through a lens of superiority, viewing them as primitive or superstitious. This perspective was used to justify control and exploitation, as traditional systems were replaced with Western legal frameworks. In Nigeria, British colonial narratives painted witchcraft as a threat to progress and order, leading to the suppression of indigenous practices. The imposition of Western laws disrupted the social fabric, marginalizing traditional healers and altering community dynamics.

Despite these challenges, witchcraft beliefs persist in modern African societies, reflecting both continuity and change. In times of social unrest, accusations of witchcraft often surge, revealing deep-seated tensions and insecurities. Witchcraft can be used as a political tool, a means of discrediting rivals or manipulating public opinion. This manipulation highlights the enduring power of belief in shaping political and social landscapes. The resurgence of witchcraft accusations in Northern Ghana during the 1990s, for example, underscores the complexities of modern life, where traditional beliefs intersect with contemporary issues.

In Rwanda, the narratives surrounding the genocide reveal the role of witchcraft as both a tool of division and a source of resilience. Stories of magical protection and curses reflect the deep cultural roots of these beliefs, even amidst unspeakable tragedy. Witchcraft offers a means of understanding and processing the horrors of conflict, providing a framework for healing and reconciliation. This chapter invites you to explore the rich and varied landscape of African witchcraft, to see beyond the stereotypes and appreciate the depth and diversity of these practices. The stories and beliefs that have shaped communities for generations continue to offer insight into the human experience, challenging us to consider the ways in which magic and reality intertwine.

WITCHCRAFT IN INDIGENOUS NORTH AMERICAN SOCIETIES

In the vast landscapes of North America, where towering forests and expansive plains meet the sky, Indigenous societies have long cultivated rich traditions steeped in spiritual and cultural significance. These societies view the world as a web of connections between the physical and spiritual realms. Within this tapestry, witchcraft is not a dark art but a testament to a deep respect for nature and the unseen. Shamanistic practices stand at the heart of many Indigenous cultures, with shamans acting as spiritual guides and healers. They possess the unique ability to traverse both worlds, using their knowledge to restore balance and harmony. Shamans draw upon the natural elements and animal spirits, invoking their power in rituals that heal and protect. Each element and spirit holds unique significance, contributing to a holistic understanding of the universe. The use of natural elements, such as herbs and stones, is intertwined with the belief in animal spirits, which serve as guides and protectors. These spirits, whether in the form of a bear, eagle, or wolf, embody qualities that are revered and emulated.

Among the Navajo, the concept of skinwalkers introduces a form of witchcraft that is as fascinating as it is feared. These individuals, known as "yee naaldlooshii," are believed to possess the ability to transform into animals or assume their traits. This power is not used for good; instead, skinwalkers are often associated with malevolent deeds and dark magic. They are figures of horror within Navajo culture, representing a corruption of the natural order. The stories of skinwalkers are more than mere folklore; they serve as warnings about the misuse of spiritual power and the consequences of breaking with tradition. In contrast, the role of "curanderos" in Latin American Indigenous cultures highlights a more benevolent aspect of witchcraft. These healers blend indigenous knowledge with spiritual practices to treat ailments of the body and spirit. They are deeply respected for their ability to cure and counsel, often using rituals that incorporate prayer, herbs, and sacred symbols. Vision quests, a rite of passage in many Indigenous cultures, reflect the spiritual journey one undertakes to gain insight and personal growth. During a vision quest, individuals seek solitude in nature, fasting and praying until they receive a vision or message from the spirit world. This practice is integral to understanding one's purpose and connection to the greater cosmos.

The arrival of European colonizers brought profound changes to Indigenous witchcraft practices. Colonial powers, driven by a desire to control and convert, often suppressed native traditions. Practices that had sustained societies for generations were labeled as heretical or pagan, leading to their prohibition. The imposition of European beliefs and systems disrupted the balance of Indigenous communities, marginalizing traditional spiritual leaders and practices. Many Indigenous peoples were forced to conceal their rituals and beliefs, blending them with Christian elements to survive. This blending of traditions resulted in a unique fusion, where Christian hymns might be sung alongside ancient chants, and biblical figures were revered alongside traditional deities. This blending, while a testament to resilience, also reflects the pressures faced by Indigenous societies to adapt and preserve their heritage in the face of external domination.

In recent years, there has been a resurgence of interest in preserving and revitalizing Indigenous witchcraft traditions. Cultural preservation programs have emerged, dedicated to safeguarding these rich heritages for future generations. Storytelling, an age-old tradition, plays a crucial role in this process, allowing elders to pass down wisdom and knowledge through narratives that captivate and educate. Modern reinterpretations and celebrations of traditional rituals have gained popularity, as communities strive to reconnect with their roots and affirm their cultural identities. These efforts are not merely about preserving the past but about embracing it as a living, evolving part of contemporary life. Festivals and gatherings celebrate traditional practices, offering a platform for education and community building. These events provide opportunities for younger generations to learn from their elders, ensuring that the wisdom of the past continues to inform the present.

As Indigenous communities work to reclaim and honor their spiritual practices, they offer a powerful reminder of the enduring relationship between humanity and the natural world. They challenge us to reflect on our own connections to the world around us, urging a deeper appreciation for the wisdom embedded in the ancient practices of those who came before.

CHAPTER 7

WITCHCRAFT AND WESTERN RELIGION

I magine standing in a grand cathedral, where flickering candles cast shadows across stone arches, and the air is thick with incense and whispered prayers. This was the heart of the Catholic Church during the Renaissance, a period of profound transformation and introspection. Yet, beneath the surface of this spiritual grandeur lay a world fraught with fear and suspicion. The Church, grappling with threats to its authority, turned its gaze toward the shadows, where whispers of heresy and witchcraft festered. In this crucible of faith and fear, the Catholic Inquisition emerged as a formidable force, determined to root out the perceived evils lurking within its fold.

WITCHCRAFT AND THE CATHOLIC INQUISITION

The establishment of the Roman Inquisition in 1542 marked a significant turning point in the Church's approach to heresy and witchcraft. This institution, distinct from the earlier medieval Inquisition, was founded under Pope Paul III, aiming to centralize and strengthen the Church's response to doctrinal threats. Its mandate extended beyond heresy, encompassing witchcraft accusations as part of a broader effort to maintain orthodoxy. The Inquisition's reach was vast, with tribunals established across Europe, each tasked with identifying and prosecuting those suspected of deviating from the Church's teachings. These tribunals employed a rigorous process of interrogation and examination, often relying on confessions extracted under duress. Accused individuals faced intense scrutiny, as inquisitors sought to uncover any evidence of diabolical activity. The procedures were designed to leave no stone unturned, reflecting the Church's determination to eradicate any threat to its spiritual authority.

Official decrees, also called papal bulls, played a pivotal role in shaping the Church's stance on witchcraft, serving as official decrees that sanctioned and guided inquisitorial actions. One of the most significant of these was *Summis desiderantes affectibus*, issued by Pope Innocent VIII in 1484. This bull, a response to a request from inquisitor Heinrich Kramer, granted explicit authority to prosecute witchcraft in Germany. It outlined the perceived dangers of witchcraft and heresy, endorsing the efforts to correct and punish those involved. The bull's issuance signified a shift in Church policy, recognizing the existence of witches and legitimizing the pursuit of their eradication. While its impact is debated, the bull undeniably contributed to the fervor of the witch hunts, providing a theological justification for the actions of inquisitors across Europe.

The theological interplay between witchcraft and Catholic doctrine further fueled the Church's actions. Witches were cast as servants of Satan, a portrayal rooted in theological interpretations of evil and sin. Augustine, a foundational figure in Christian theology, had long warned against the dangers of sorcery, viewing it as a perversion of divine order. Thomas Aquinas, later building upon Augustine's work, articulated a detailed demonology that positioned witches as agents of the devil. This theological framework provided a powerful lens through which the Church viewed witchcraft, reinforcing the perception of witches as embodiments of malevolence. The Church's teachings emphasized the cosmic battle between good and evil, with witches portrayed as pawns in Satan's grand design. This narrative not only justified but necessitated the Church's efforts to combat witchcraft, framing it as a spiritual duty to protect the faithful.

Significant trials conducted by the Inquisition serve as stark examples of how these beliefs manifested in practice. In Spain, the trial of Maria de la Cueva stands out as a case that exemplified the Inquisition's reach and influence. Accused of witchcraft in the late 16th century, Maria faced an inquisition that was thorough and relentless. Her trial, marked by intense interrogation and public spectacle, resulted in a conviction that underscored the Inquisition's commitment to its cause. Similarly, the Basque witch trials of the early 17th century highlight the Inquisition's role in shaping regional perceptions of witchcraft. These trials, conducted in the borderlands of Spain and France, saw hundreds accused and many executed, leaving a lasting impact on the communities involved. The trials were characterized by their scale and intensity, reflecting the Inquisition's determination to root out witchcraft wherever it was perceived to flourish.

In Italy, the Inquisition's impact on witchcraft perceptions was profound. Italian inquisitors, operating under the auspices of the Roman Inquisition, pursued cases with a zeal that mirrored the broader European trend. The trials conducted in regions like Venice and Milan were notable for their thoroughness and severity, as the Church sought to assert its dominance in the face of growing secular influence. These trials often targeted individuals accused of engaging in witchcraft alongside heretical practices, reinforcing the intertwined nature of these perceived threats. The outcomes of these trials varied, but they collectively contributed to a climate of fear and control, shaping societal attitudes toward witchcraft and the Church's authority.

As you reflect on these historical narratives, consider how the intersection of religion, power, and fear shaped the lives of those accused of witchcraft. The Inquisition's legacy, marked by its pursuit of orthodoxy and control, offers a window into the complexities of faith and authority in a world teetering on the edge of transformation.

PROTESTANT REFORMATION AND WITCH HUNTS

In the throes of the 16th century, Europe found itself at a crossroads of belief and power, as the Protestant Reformation ignited a seismic shift in religious thought and practice. The Reformation, spearheaded by figures like Martin Luther and John Calvin, challenged the Catholic Church's authority, seeking to purify Christian doctrine and eliminate perceived corruptions. This religious upheaval not only redefined spiritual landscapes but also heightened fears of witchcraft, casting a long shadow over European society. The reformers, intent on establishing a new orthodoxy, saw witchcraft as a tangible manifestation of evil and a remnant of Catholic "idolatry" and superstition. In their quest for religious purity, they associated witchcraft with the old Church's rituals and beliefs, branding it as a diabolical force that needed to be eradicated.

Martin Luther, one of the Reformation's most influential voices, played a pivotal role in shaping Protestant views on witchcraft. His sermons were imbued with vivid imagery and emotional appeal, painting witches as emissaries of the Devil. Luther's rhetoric was powerful, designed to rally his followers and fortify the nascent Protestant faith against external threats. By framing witchcraft as a direct affront to God's order, Luther amplified the fear and suspicion surrounding those accused of practicing it. Similarly, John Calvin, another towering figure of the Reformation, wielded his intellectual might against the perceived threat of witchcraft. In his seminal work, the *Institutes of the Chris-*

tian Religion, Calvin articulated the spiritual dangers posed by witches, emphasizing the need for vigilance and purity. His writings served as a theological foundation for Protestant communities, reinforcing the belief that witchcraft was a grave sin that endangered both the individual and the collective soul.

The impact of Protestant sermons and religious texts on public perception was profound and deeply influential. In a time when literacy was limited, sermons were a primary means of communication and instruction. Protestant leaders used the pulpit to warn against the insidious nature of witchcraft, instilling fear and mistrust among their congregations. These fiery orations, coupled with widely circulated pamphlets, fueled a climate of anxiety and suspicion. The notion that witches were actively working to subvert the divine order permeated the cultural consciousness, leading to an increase in accusations and prosecutions. This period saw a proliferation of witch hunts across Protestant territories, each case reflecting the complex interplay of religion, power, and fear.

In Germany, the Württemberg witch hunts exemplify the fervor with which Protestant communities pursued alleged witches. These hunts, driven by a combination of religious zeal and local tensions, resulted in numerous trials and executions. The region, already a hotbed of religious conflict, became a crucible for witchcraft accusations, as communities sought to purify themselves by rooting out perceived evil. The influence of King James VI of Scotland further illustrates the intersection of Protestant belief and witch trials. His treatise, *Daemonologie*, published in 1597, provided a detailed account of witchcraft and its dangers, legitimizing the prosecution of witches in Scotland and beyond. James's work was instrumental in shaping attitudes toward witchcraft, reinforcing the perception of witches as agents of chaos and disorder.

Scandinavia's Lutheran Church also played a significant role in the witch trials that swept through the region. The Church's emphasis on confession and repentance resonated with communities eager to cleanse themselves of sin and impurity. Witch trials in places like Finland and Sweden reflected this fervor, with accusations often leading to severe punishments. The trials were characterized by their intensity and scope, as communities sought to rid themselves of the perceived threat posed by witches. The Lutheran Church's involvement in these prosecutions underscores the broader trend of religious institutions leveraging witch trials to assert control and reinforce doctrinal conformity.

The approaches to witchcraft taken by Catholic and Protestant authorities, while sharing underlying themes of fear and control, differed in notable ways. Catholic trials, often influenced by the Inquisition, emphasized the identification and eradication of heresy, with a focus on theological conformity. In contrast, Protestant trials placed greater emphasis on individual confession and repentance, reflecting the Reformation's focus on personal faith and salvation. The severity of punishments also varied, with Protestant regions often imposing harsher penalties for those found guilty of witchcraft. This divergence highlights the nuanced ways in which religious beliefs and institutional structures shaped the prosecution of witchcraft during this tumultuous period.

CHAPTER 8

THE ROLE OF FEAR AND SUPERSTITION

P icture a bustling medieval town square, where whispers of disease spread faster than the sickness itself. In the dim candlelight of a local tavern, villagers exchange fearful glances, murmuring about the mysterious deaths ravaging their community. The specter of plague looms large, an invisible menace that defies understanding, leaving people desperate for answers and someone to blame. This fear, palpable and pervasive, sets the stage for one of history's most insidious scapegoating mechanisms: the witch hunt. As you delve into this chapter, consider how the invisible horrors of disease shaped the human impulse to find tangible culprits in a bid to regain control over chaos.

THE ROLE OF PLAGUES IN WITCHCRAFT ACCUSATIONS

The infamous Black Death of 1348 serves as a stark reminder of how cataclysmic events can redefine societies. This plague decimated Europe, wiping out between one-third and one-half of the population within a few years, leaving a trail of devastation and despair. The psychological impact was profound, as communities grappled with the sudden loss and destruction of their world. In the wake of such trauma, the search for scapegoats became a coping mechanism, a way to make sense of the senseless. As a result, witch-hunts intensified during this period, reflecting a desperate attempt to identify and eliminate perceived threats to social stability. The fear of recurrence kept the specter of witchcraft alive, fueling further suspicion and persecution.

The correlation between disease outbreaks and witchcraft accusations did not end with the Black Death. In colonial America, smallpox outbreaks created similar conditions of fear and uncertainty. Communities, already struggling with the challenges of a new world, found themselves besieged by unseen forces that threatened their very survival. The fear of disease and the unknown led to increased witch trials, as people sought explanations and solutions in the realm of the supernatural. The idea that witches could wield the power to curse and control disease resonated with those looking for answers, making them easy targets for blame.

Historical accounts abound with examples of how witches were unjustly linked to the spread of disease. Trial records from across Europe reveal accusations of witches poisoning wells, a crime believed to have brought pestilence to entire towns. These accusations, often based on superstition rather than evidence, highlight the extent to which fear overshadowed reason. In rural communities, witches were also blamed for cursing livestock, leading to food shortages and further social unrest. The idea of witches as malevolent agents capable of inflicting harm on both people and their livelihoods took hold, reinforcing the need for community vigilance and retribution.

Religious interpretations played a significant role in framing plagues as divine punishment, giving weight to witchcraft accusations. Sermons delivered from pulpits across Europe equated disease outbreaks with sin and moral decay, suggesting that witches, as agents of the Devil, were instruments of divine wrath. This narrative provided a theological framework that supported the persecution of witches, casting them as scapegoats in a cosmic struggle between good and evil. The belief that witches could harness dark forces to unleash disease aligned with theological narratives, reinforcing the idea that rooting out witchcraft was both a moral and spiritual imperative.

The human tendency to seek scapegoats during times of crisis is a reflection of the deep-seated psychological need for control and understanding. In the face of intangible disasters, tangible culprits offer a semblance of order amidst chaos. Community leaders, aware of this dynamic, often exploited fear to maintain control, using witch trials as a means to assert authority and reinforce social norms. These leaders understood that a shared enemy could unite a fractured community, channeling fear and frustration into collective action. This manipulation of fear not only preserved their power but also perpetuated the cycle of suspicion and persecution.

SUPERSTITIONS AND THEIR HISTORICAL ROOTS

Imagine the flicker of candlelight casting long shadows on the walls of a small village house. Inside, an elderly woman clutches an amulet, whispering incantations to ward off the evil eye. This ancient belief, that a malevolent glare could bring misfortune, has roots extending far back into antiquity. The evil eye was feared across cultures, seen as a force capable of causing illness, bad luck, or even death. To counteract its effects, people turned to protective charms, such as the hamsa or the blue-eye talisman, believing these objects held the power to deflect the gaze and protect the wearer from harm. Such superstitions were not confined to any single society but were shared across the Mediterranean, the Middle East, and beyond, each with its own variations and adaptations.

The lore surrounding witches' familiars—animals believed to assist witches in their magical endeavors—is another example of how superstitions shaped perceptions of witchcraft. These companions, often depicted as cats, toads, or owls, were thought to be demonic spirits in disguise, serving as both helpers and spies for their witch masters. Legends of these familiars permeated folklore, reinforcing the belief that witches were never alone in their nefarious deeds. The presence of animals in witchcraft accusations added a layer of fear and mystique, as even the most mundane creature could be seen as a supernatural accomplice. This belief reflected the broader human tendency to attribute unexplained events to the workings of unseen forces, providing a narrative that connected the natural and supernatural worlds.

Superstitions provided a framework for justifying witchcraft accusations, often transforming fear into action. In the courtroom, talismans and amulets found in a suspect's possession could serve as damning evidence of witchcraft. These items, whether intended for protection or healing, were reinterpreted as tools of malice, used to curse or enchant. Stories of crop failures attributed to hexes and curses further illustrate how superstition fueled accusations. When harvests were poor or livestock fell ill, it was easier to blame a neighbor suspected of witchcraft than to acknowledge natural causes or human error. Nighttime gatherings, another staple of witch lore, were seen as proof of witches' secret rituals and pacts with dark forces. The cover of darkness, coupled with the mystery of the night, intensified suspicions, making these gatherings prime evidence in witch trials.

The cultural differences in superstitions reveal how local beliefs shaped the narratives surrounding witchcraft.

In Celtic regions, fairy folklore played a significant role in witchcraft accusations. Fairies, with their capricious and often mischievous nature, were believed to interact with humans, sometimes bestowing gifts or curses. This belief in a hidden world of spirits influenced the perception of witches as intermediaries with these otherworldly beings. In Scandinavia, trolls—a mythical race known for their trickery and connection to the natural world—were similarly linked to witchcraft. The belief that witches could summon trolls to do their bidding added a layer of complexity to the witchcraft narrative, intertwining human and mythical fears.

Even in modern times, remnants of these superstitions continue to influence contemporary culture. Halloween, celebrated with costumes and carved pumpkins, has its roots in ancient practices meant to ward off evil spirits. The tradition of dressing up in disguise stems from the belief that wearing a mask would confuse malevolent entities, preventing them from recognizing and harming the wearer. Similarly, the continued belief in unlucky omens, such as black cats crossing one's path, harks back to witch lore, where animals were often seen as harbingers of misfortune. These superstitions, though often dismissed as quaint or entertaining, reflect the enduring power of narratives that tap into our deepest fears and curiosities.

As you consider these historical roots, think about how these superstitions might still subtly shape your own perceptions and behaviors. The legacy of these beliefs, woven into the fabric of cultural consciousness, endures in ways both seen and unseen. As you move forward, keep in mind how the narratives of the past continue to echo in the present, influencing attitudes and actions. With this understanding, the exploration of witchcraft's historical and cultural impact deepens, inviting further reflection on the complexities of belief and the human experience.

CHAPTER 9
WITCH TRIALS IN EUROPE AND THE NEW WORLD

THE PENDLE WITCH TRIALS

I magine the rolling hills of Lancashire in the early 17th century, where the air is thick with anticipation and suspicion. The year is 1612, and a series of events is about to unfold in the forest of Pendle, which would leave an indelible mark on history. The Pendle Witch Trials, one of the most famous witch trials in England, occurred against a backdrop of social, political, and religious upheaval. This was a time when King James I, who had ascended to the English throne in 1603, held a deep-seated fear of witchcraft. His treatise, "Daemonologie," published in 1597, reflected his belief in a world where witches conspired with demons. This text fueled his paranoia and laid the groundwork for the prosecution of those accused of witchcraft. The influence of King James I cannot be under-stated; his fear of witches permeated through the societal fabric, shaping perceptions and igniting witch hunts across the land.

In Lancashire, the local tensions were palpable. The area was rife with economic hardship and religious conflict, exacerbated by the harshness of the upland cattle and cloth economy. Disputes over resources and property were common, leading to divisions within parish communities. These tensions, coupled with family rivalries, created a volatile environment ripe for witchcraft accusations. The religious divide between Catholics and Protestants further fueled suspicion, as neighbors turned against each other in an atmosphere of mistrust.

The Pendle Witch Trials began in March 1612, when Alizon Device, a local woman, was accused of causing harm through witchcraft. Her confession set off a chain of events that would lead to the arrest of many others, culminating in a series of trials held at Lancaster Assizes. The legal proceedings were marked by several deviations from standard practices, most notably the use of child witnesses. Jennet Device, a nine-year-old girl, played a pivotal role in the trials. Her testimony against her own family members was both shocking and compelling, swaying the court with her detailed accounts of witchcraft activities. Jennet's involvement highlights the desperation and fear that characterized these trials, as even the innocence of childhood was manipulated in the pursuit of justice.

Magistrate Roger Nowell was another key figure in the Pendle Witch Trials. His zealous pursuit of witches reflected the broader societal fear of witchcraft, as well as the influence of King James I's beliefs. Nowell's role was instrumental in the gathering of evidence and the prosecution of the accused. The trials themselves were a spectacle, with large crowds gathering to witness the proceedings. The evidence presented was often flimsy, relying heavily on hearsay and testimonies from neighbors and community members. Allegations of causing illness and death through witchcraft were common, with the accused often blamed for misfortunes that had befallen their neighbors, such as the death of livestock or the failure of crops. The testimonies were filled with vivid accounts of supernatural occurrences, weaving a narrative that both frightened and fascinated those who listened.

The outcomes of the Pendle Witch Trials were as tragic as they were significant. Ten individuals were executed as a result of the trials, their deaths serving as a grim reminder of the power of fear and superstition. The impact of these trials extended beyond the immediate community, shaping public perception of witchcraft in England. The Pendle Witch Trials became a symbol of the dangers of unchecked hysteria, highlighting the ease with which ordinary people could be swept up in a tide of accusation and retribution. The trials also influenced subsequent witch hunts, as the methods and rhetoric employed were mirrored in later prosecutions.

The legacy of the Pendle Witch Trials is complex, serving as both a cautionary tale and a window into the societal dynamics of early 17th-century England. These events remind us of the thin line between belief and fear, and the consequences that can arise when that line is crossed.

THE SALEM WITCH TRIALS: MYTH VS. REALITY

In 17th-century colonial Massachusetts, the very air seemed charged with tension, as if the land itself held its breath. The Puritans, who had settled in this new world seeking religious freedom, were a community deeply bound by their faith. Their belief system was stringent, emphasizing the constant presence of the Devil and the ever-looming threat of sin. This was a society where the fear of eternal damnation was tangible, influencing daily life and governance. The Puritan's worldview was one of strict moral codes and an unwavering belief that the Devil was constantly at work, seeking to corrupt and destroy. This pervasive fear created a fertile ground for suspicion and distrust, where whispers of witchcraft could ignite the flames of hysteria.

Adding to these religious tensions was the economic and political instability within the Massachusetts Bay Colony. The region was still recovering from the aftermath of King Philip's War, a brutal conflict with Native American tribes that had left deep scars on the land and its people. The war had strained resources, deepened mistrust, and left many communities vulnerable. It was a time of uncertainty and fear, where the boundaries between friend and foe were blurred. Political strife within the colony further exacerbated these tensions, as factions vied for power and influence. This instability created an environment where fear and suspicion could easily take root, setting the stage for the events that would unfold in Salem.

The Salem Witch Trials began in 1692 in the small village of Salem, where a group of young girls, including Betty Parris and Abigail Williams, began exhibiting strange behaviors. Their fits and convulsions were attributed to witchcraft, sparking a wave of accusations that quickly spread throughout the community. These initial accusations were both a catalyst and a reflection of the underlying tensions within Salem. Reverend Samuel Parris, the village's minister, played a significant role in the trials. His own daughter was among the afflicted, and his sermons fanned the flames of fear and paranoia. Parris's influence was profound, as he used the pulpit to warn of the Devil's presence and the need for vigilance against his agents.

Judge Samuel Sewall, another key figure in the trials, was one of the judges presiding over the court proceedings. The trials were marred by the use of spectral evidence, a controversial form of testimony that allowed accusers to claim they were being tormented by the specters, or spirits, of the accused. This type of evidence was highly subjective and relied heavily on the accuser's word, making it a powerful tool for those seeking to manipulate the trials for personal gain. The use of spectral evidence was divisive, with some clergy, like Increase Mather, eventually arguing against it. Mather's involvement and subsequent recantation highlighted the growing concern over the fairness and legitimacy of the trials. His objections, along with public outcry, eventually led to a shift in the proceedings, as the court began to question the validity of such evidence.

Despite the gravity of the Salem Witch Trials, several myths have persisted, shaping public perception of these events. One of the most pervasive myths is that those accused of witchcraft were burned at the stake. In reality, the executions were carried out by hanging, a grim but common method of execution at the time. This misconception has been fueled by dramatic retellings and popular culture, distorting the historical record. Another misunderstanding surrounds the role of ergot poisoning as a possible explanation for the girls' afflictions. While some historians have suggested that ergot, a fungus that grows on rye and produces hallucinogenic effects, may have contributed to the symptoms, there is little concrete evidence to support this theory. The reality of the trials is complex, shaped by a multitude of factors beyond a single cause.

The aftermath of the Salem Witch Trials left a profound impact on the community and the wider world. In the years following the trials, many of those accused were eventually pardoned, as the colony grappled with the injustice of the events. Public apologies were made, and compensation was offered to the families of the accused, reflecting a desire to heal the wounds inflicted by the hysteria. The trials also prompted changes in legal standards, as the use of spectral evidence was discredited, leading to reforms that emphasized the need for tangible proof in court proceedings. This shift marked a turning point in American legal history,

influencing the development of legal principles that prioritized due process and the rights of the accused.

The legacy of the Salem Witch Trials extends far beyond
the borders of Massachusetts, leaving an indelible mark on
American cultural and legal history. The trials serve as a
cautionary tale about the dangers of mass hysteria and the
consequences of unchecked fear. They remind us of the
importance of justice, reason, and compassion in the face of
societal panic.

CHAPTER 10
CASE STUDIES OF LESSER-KNOWN WITCH TRIALS

THE MORA WITCH TRIAL IN SWEDEN

I n the quiet, snow-draped village of Mora, nestled in the heart of Sweden, a chill far colder than the winter air descended upon its people in the late 17th century. This chill was not of nature but born of fear and suspicion. It was a time when the whispers of witchcraft could spiral into hysteria, gripping entire communities. Mora, a seemingly tranquil settlement, became the epicenter of what would be remembered as one of Sweden's most notorious witch trials. To understand how this trial unfolded, we must delve into the socio-political landscape of 17th-century Sweden, a nation reeling from the aftermath of the Thirty Years' War. This prolonged conflict had left its mark on Europe, and Sweden was no exception. The war had drained resources, strained communities, and sowed seeds of uncertainty across the land. Amidst these tensions, Lutheran orthodoxy took a firm hold, shaping public attitudes and intertwining with traditional beliefs. The Church, a pillar of societal stability, wielded significant influence, and its doctrines permeated everyday life. This religious backdrop played a crucial role in molding perceptions, as witchcraft was increasingly viewed not just as heresy but as an existential threat to the moral fabric of society.

As the witch craze took root in 1668, Mora found itself swept up in the tide of accusations and fear. The trial proceedings were marked by the involvement of Chief Judge Laurentius Hornaeus, a figure whose presence would become synonymous with the Mora witch trials. Hornaeus, operating under the mandate of the Swedish crown, navigated the complex interplay of fear, belief, and justice. His role was pivotal, as he oversaw the interrogation and prosecution of those accused. The testimonies of children, a shocking yet common element in these trials, played a crucial role. Children, often coerced or manipulated, recounted vivid tales of abductions and gatherings at Blåkulla—a mythical witches' sabbath. Their testimonies, despite the dubious nature of such evidence, were given considerable weight in the proceedings, reflecting the desperate need to root out perceived evil. The use of physical evidence and confessions obtained under duress further complicated the legal landscape. Swedish law, typically resistant to such methods, found itself influenced by

Continental practices, where forced confessions were not uncommon. This departure from established legal norms underscores the intensity of the witchcraft panic that gripped the region.

The accusations themselves were steeped in cultural beliefs and folklore. Allegations centered around the infamous Blåkulla, a place where witches were said to gather for their unholy rites. This imagery, drawn from deepseated superstitions, painted a picture of malevolence that resonated with the fears of the time. The tales of Blåkulla, though fantastical, held a powerful sway over the collective imagination, fueling the frenzy that enveloped Mora. Folklore and superstition, potent forces in shaping community fears, were skillfully manipulated, turning neighbor against neighbor in a desperate bid for survival. This atmosphere of dread and suspicion was not unique to Mora but reflected a broader societal trend, where the boundaries of reality and myth blurred, leading to tragic consequences.

The outcomes of the Mora witch trial were devastating and far-reaching. The execution of 14 individuals cast a long shadow over the village, serving as both punishment and deterrent. These executions, carried out with grim efficiency, were meant to cleanse the community of its perceived corruption. However, the impact extended beyond the immediate loss of life. The trial's influence reverberated throughout Sweden, setting a precedent for subsequent witch hunts and reinforcing the power dynamics at play. The legacy of the Mora witch trial lingers, a stark reminder of the destructive power of fear and the human capacity for scapegoating in times of crisis.

WITCH HUNTS IN SCOTLAND: A FORGOTTEN HISTORY

In the rugged landscapes of Scotland, where mist veils the rolling hills and ancient castles stand sentinel against time, the echoes of witch hunts still linger. The socio-political environment during the witch hunts was shaped by profound changes, particularly the Reformation's sweeping influence. This movement, which established the Church of Scotland, altered the religious and cultural fabric of the nation. The Church of Scotland, with its strong Calvinist roots, emphasized moral purity and a literal interpretation of the Bible. This doctrinal rigidity created an atmosphere ripe for witch hunts, as any deviation from religious norms was viewed with suspicion. Local lairds and community leaders played a significant role in this dynamic. They often used witch hunts to assert power and maintain order within their territories. The lairds, acting as both enforcers and beneficiaries of the Church's influence, found in witch trials a convenient tool for dealing with dissent and unrest. This interplay of religion and power fueled a climate where accusations could quickly spiral into full-blown hunts, driven by both genuine belief and opportunistic motives.

Among the notable witch trials in Scotland, the North Berwick trials stand out for their connection to King James VI. These trials, which took place between 1590 and 1592, were not just about rooting out witches; they were deeply entwined with the king's own experiences and beliefs. King James VI, having encountered a fierce storm while sailing from Denmark with his bride, became convinced that witchcraft was responsible. His personal involvement in the trials lent them a unique intensity, as he sought to root out the supposed conspiracy against him. The trials led to the execution of many, their confessions extracted through torture and intimidation. Local folklore played a significant role in shaping the accusations, with stories of witches raising storms and communing with the devil feeding the hysteria. Similarly, the Paisley witch trials were marked by the use of local legends and superstitions. These trials often revolved around accusations of causing harm through magical means, with the community's fears and beliefs amplifying the charges. The trial of Isobel Gowdie, another significant case, is particularly remarkable for her detailed confessions. Her vivid descriptions of witchcraft activities, which included interactions with fairy folk and attendance at witches' sabbaths, provide a fascinating insight into the intersection of folklore and fear. Gowdie's confessions, though likely coerced, reflect the rich tapestry of Scottish cultural beliefs and the power of narrative in shaping reality.

The legal and religious frameworks in Scotland played a crucial role in the conduct of witch trials. The Witchcraft Act of 1563, passed under Mary Queen of Scots, made witchcraft a capital offense, setting the stage for the persecution that followed. This act, rooted in the desire to enforce moral purity and religious conformity, provided the legal basis for trials across the country. Kirk sessions, local church courts, were instrumental in investigating and prosecuting witchcraft cases. These sessions, often composed of community members and clergy, served as both judge and jury, reflecting the deep intertwining of religious and legal authority. The Kirk sessions' role in the trials underscores the pervasive influence of the Church in everyday life, where spiritual and temporal matters were inseparable. Their proceedings, which could include public confessions and penance, highlight the community's involvement in the process, where collective fear and belief drove the machinery of justice.

The legacy of the Scottish witch hunts is complex, leaving a lasting imprint on cultural identity and historical memory. By the late 17th century, the fervor of witch hunts began to wane, as skepticism and legal reforms took hold. The decline was marked by a growing awareness of the injustices perpetrated and a shift towards more rational approaches to justice. Efforts to commemorate the victims of these hunts have emerged over time, with memorials and historical reflections serving as reminders of the past. The influence of Scottish witch trials extends into contemporary cultural narratives and folklore, where tales of witches continue to captivate the imagination. These stories, steeped in history and myth, reflect the enduring fascination with the supernatural and the human tendency to seek scapegoats in times of uncertainty. As we move forward, the lessons from Scotland's witch hunts remind us of the dangers of unchecked power and the importance of compassion and understanding in the face of fear.

As we move forward, the next chapter will delve into the intersection of witchcraft and law, exploring how legal systems have shaped and been shaped by societal views on witchcraft.

CHAPTER II
WITCHCRAFT AND EARLY LAW

P icture a courtroom in the medieval era, where the air is thick with the scent of wax and parchment, and the eyes of the gathered crowd are fixed on the accused. Here, the stakes are life and death, and the law is both a shield and a sword. This setting is not merely a backdrop for drama but a real stage where history unfolded, as legal systems grappled with the enigmatic and fearful phenomenon of witchcraft. The legal frameworks that targeted witchcraft were not born overnight. They evolved over centuries, reflecting the shifting tides of power, religion, and societal norms. These frameworks laid the groundwork for trials that would claim the lives of thousands across Europe, leaving a legacy of fear and confusion in their wake.

LEGAL SYSTEMS AND WITCHCRAFT ACCUSATIONS

The development of legal codes specifically addressing witchcraft began to take shape in the early medieval period. One of the earliest examples is the Lex Salica, a legal code of the Salian Franks. This code, rooted in the customs of a Germanic tribe, outlined penalties for various crimes, including sorcery. It established a foundation for how witchcraft was perceived and prosecuted in early medieval Europe. The Lex Salica's influence extended beyond its immediate context, shaping subsequent legal developments across the continent. It reflected the belief that witchcraft was not just a personal sin but a societal threat that required regulation and control.

As centuries passed, the legal landscape continued to evolve, culminating in the Constitutio Criminalis Carolina, enacted in 1532. This comprehensive legal code was approved by the Reichstag of the Holy Roman Empire and promulgated by Emperor Charles V. It marked a pivotal moment in the codification of criminal law, including provisions for witchcraft. The Carolina, as it was commonly known, provided a detailed framework for the prosecution of crimes, emphasizing the importance of procedure and evidence. It outlined the process of "inquisition," a methodical approach to determining guilt or innocence through official inquests and, if necessary, judicial torture. While torture was considered a last resort, the Carolina specified conditions under which it could be employed, requiring legally sufficient indication of guilt, akin to modern "probable cause." This legal standard reflected an attempt to balance justice with the need for public order, a delicate equilibrium that often tipped in favor of harsh measures.

Judicial practices in witchcraft trials were often characterized by their severity and reliance on confessions. Accusations were pursued with a zeal that sometimes bordered on fervor, and the methods employed to extract confessions were both varied and brutal. The infamous "swimming test," for example, was one such method. Accused individuals were bound and thrown into water with the belief that the innocent would sink, while witches would float, rejected by the pure element. This test, cruel and arbitrary, exemplified the lengths to which authorities would go to prove guilt. The outcomes were often predetermined, as fear and superstition overshadowed reason and fairness.

The distinction between inquisitorial and accusatorial systems played a crucial role in these trials. Inquisitorial systems, prevalent in much of continental Europe, were marked by a centralized investigation process, where the judge actively sought evidence and questioned the accused. This system allowed for a more controlled environment but also concentrated power in the hands of the judiciary, leading to potential abuses. In contrast, accusatorial systems, more common in England, relied on the presentation of evidence by opposing parties, with the judge serving as an arbiter. This approach emphasized the adversarial nature of the trial, where the burden of proof lay with the accuser. However, both systems were susceptible to manipulation, particularly when fear and prejudice clouded judgment.

The prosecution of witchcraft often found itself at the intersection of secular and ecclesiastical courts, leading to jurisdictional conflicts and overlapping authorities. In Southern Europe, the Inquisition played a significant role in witch trials. As an institution of the Catholic Church, the Inquisition sought to root out heresy and maintain doctrinal purity. Its involvement in witchcraft prosecutions highlighted the religious dimensions of these trials, where spiritual and temporal concerns intertwined. The overlap between church law and state law created a complex legal landscape, where the boundaries of authority were often blurred. Secular courts, increasingly influenced by emerging nation-states, sought to assert their jurisdiction over matters of public order, including witchcraft. This dual system of governance reflected the broader tensions between church and state, with each vying for control over the pursuit of justice.

The codification of witchcraft laws in England and Scotland further illustrates the evolving legal responses to witchcraft. The Witchcraft Act of 1542 in England marked the first instance of witchcraft being codified as a criminal offense punishable by death. This act, under the jurisdiction of civil courts, signaled a shift from ecclesiastical to secular prosecution. Although it was repealed in 1547, its influence lingered, leading to subsequent acts that reinforced the criminalization of witchcraft. The Scottish Witchcraft Act of 1563 followed a similar trajectory,

reflecting the broader European trend toward legal codification and prosecution of witchcraft. These acts not only
shaped the legal landscape but also reflected societal attitudes toward witchcraft, reinforcing the view of it as a
threat to both spiritual and social order.

THE TRIAL OF URBAIN GRANDIER

In the early 17th century, the bustling town of Loudun in
France became the stage for a dramatic and controversial
witch trial, centered around Urbain Grandier, a charismatic
and outspoken Catholic priest. Grandier was known for his
eloquence and his defiant stance against ecclesiastical
authority, which earned him both admirers and enemies.
His reputation as a controversial figure in the community
was further fueled by his alleged romantic liaisons and his
tendency to clash with local authorities. In a time when the
Catholic Church wielded immense power, Grandier's
refusal to conform made him a target for those seeking to
assert control. The political climate in France, under the
influence of Cardinal Richelieu, was one of centralization
and consolidation of power. Richelieu, the chief minister to
King Louis XIII, sought to strengthen the monarchy by
curbing the influence of independent towns and rebellious
factions. In this environment, Loudun, with its independent streak and Grandier's defiance, posed a challenge to
Richelieu's vision of a unified France under royal control.

Against this backdrop, the accusations against Grandier
emerged, painting a picture of dark intrigue and supernat-

ural forces. The charges were grave: possession and pacts with demons, accusations that held immense weight in a deeply religious society. The catalyst for these allegations was a series of bizarre events at the Ursuline convent in Loudun, where several nuns claimed to be possessed by evil spirits. Their symptoms included convulsions, strange utterances, and accusations that Grandier had bewitched them. These testimonies, given by nuns who had taken vows of chastity and obedience, were seen as credible, adding fuel to the fire of suspicion. The nuns' accusations were vivid and detailed, describing visions of Grandier consorting with demons and orchestrating their downfall. Such claims were not uncommon in an era where the line between the spiritual and the supernatural was often blurred, and where the fear of demonic influence pervaded everyday life.

The trial proceedings against Urbain Grandier were marked by irregularities and a lack of credible evidence, yet they unfolded with a fervor that reflected the intense societal and political pressures of the time. The role of Father Tranquille, a Capuchin friar, was pivotal in the case. He conducted exorcisms at the convent, interpreting the nuns' convulsions and outbursts as evidence of possession. His involvement lent a veneer of religious legitimacy to the proceedings, though his methods and conclusions were far from impartial. The trial relied heavily on coerced confessions, extracted under duress and torture, a common practice in witch trials across Europe. Despite the flimsy evidence, the court pressed on, determined to reach a

verdict that would satisfy both religious and political inter-
ests. The lack of credible evidence was overshadowed by
the dramatic testimonies and the public spectacle of the
exorcisms, which captivated the local populace and fueled
the narrative of Grandier's guilt.

The impact of Urbain Grandier's trial and subsequent
execution was profound, resonating far beyond the borders
of Loudun. Grandier was burned at the stake, a fate
reserved for those deemed irredeemably corrupt and
dangerous to society. His execution was not just a punishment for alleged sorcery but a demonstration of the power
dynamics at play. It served as a warning to others who
might challenge the established order. The trial highlighted
the intersection between religion, politics, and law, where
personal vendettas and political ambitions often dictated
the course of justice. Richelieu's involvement, though indi-
rect, underscored the use of witchcraft accusations as a tool
for political consolidation. Grandier's execution silenced a
vocal critic of the church and state, reinforcing the message
that dissent would not be tolerated.

Reflecting on the trial's legacy, it becomes clear that the
case of Urbain Grandier was not an isolated incident but
part of a broader pattern of witchcraft prosecutions in
France and beyond. It exemplified the use of witchcraft
trials to settle scores, enforce conformity, and maintain
control. The trial also served as a precursor to the Enlightenment's challenges to superstition and the eventual
decline of witch hunts in Europe. It remains a powerful
reminder of the capacity for fear and power to shape justice

in ways that can lead to tragic outcomes. The story of Urbain Grandier, with its blend of intrigue, politics, and religion, continues to captivate and caution, offering insights into the complexities of human nature and the societies we build.

CHAPTER 12
WITCHCRAFT IN ART

WITCHES IN RENAISSANCE ART

During the Renaissance (14th to 17th Century), a period marked by a flourishing of arts and humanist ideals, the figure of the witch emerged vividly on canvas and in engravings. Artists like Albrecht Dürer captured the zeitgeist with works such as "The Witch" around the year 1500, where symbolic elements spoke volumes about societal fears and curiosities. Dürer's witch, often depicted in motion, embodies not just the supernatural but the anxieties of a world grappling with the unknown. As the printing press gained momentum, these images spread widely, fueling both fascination and dread. The dissemination of witch imagery through prints allowed for a shared visual language that could communicate complex ideas about morality, power, and the supernatural to a broader audience, reinforcing the cultural narratives surrounding witchcraft.

Renaissance art was rich with iconography that portrayed witches in various guises, reflecting the cultural meanings and fears of the time. Broomsticks and cauldrons became synonymous with the witch, symbols of both flight and transformation. These items, charged with magical connotations, depicted witches as beings who transgressed the natural order. Animal familiars, particularly cats and owls, accompanied these figures, symbolizing the witches' connection to the animal world and their supposed ability to command its creatures. Images of witches' sabbaths depicted gatherings where witches were imagined to partake in unholy rites, feeding the narrative of witchcraft as a sinister and collective threat. Through these symbols, art communicated a potent mix of fear and fascination, inviting viewers to ponder the boundaries between the seen and unseen.

Notable artists of the Renaissance, such as Hans Baldung Grien of Germany who lived from around 1484 to 1545, contributed significantly to the portrayal of witches, with a series of paintings that explored themes of tempta-tion and vice. Baldung's works often depicted witches in dynamic and unsettling compositions, capturing the tension between allure and danger. Hieronymus Bosch, a Dutch painter renowned for his fantastical depictions, infused his art with surreal elements, presenting witches within dreamlike landscapes that blurred the lines between reality and fantasy. These artists used witchcraft imagery to explore the complexities of human nature, illustrating the temptations and moral struggles that defined the human condition.

Witchcraft imagery in Renaissance art also intersected with contemporary views on gender and morality. Female witches, as depicted in art, were often portrayed as embodiments of temptation, their very presence a moral lesson on the dangers of vice and the consequences of sin. These portrayals reflected broader societal anxieties about the role of women and their perceived ability to disrupt social order. Witches became symbols of both allure and treachery, serving as cautionary figures in a world that was negotiating its values and beliefs. Through this lens, art became a medium for exploring the themes of sin and redemption, using the figure of the witch to challenge and reflect the moral codes of the time.

WITCHES IN SHAKESPEAREAN DRAMA

As the candles flicker and shadows dance across the wooden stage, the eerie chant of the "weird sisters" echoes through the air, setting a tone of supernatural unease. This is the opening scene of Shakespeare's *Macbeth* from around 1606, where the witches conjure a world teetering on the edge of chaos and ambition. Their presence is a harbinger of doom, weaving prophecies that ignite Macbeth's latent desires and drive him towards a path of destruction. The witches, often referred to as "weird sisters," are more than mere characters; they are the embodiment of fate and destiny. Their prophecies, laden with ambiguity, stir Macbeth's ambitions, pushing him to seize a future fraught with peril. As Macbeth grapples with his choices, the witches' influence looms large, their words echoing in his actions and decisions. They symbolize the unpredictable forces of fate, guiding and misleading in equal measure, leaving audiences to ponder the delicate balance between destiny and free will.

Shakespeare's portrayal of witches in *Macbeth* is rooted in the cultural context of his time, reflecting the prevalent fears and beliefs surrounding witchcraft. The early 17th century was a period of intense religious and political turmoil. King James VI of Scotland, who later became King James I of England, a monarch with a well-documented fascination with witchcraft, had ascended the English throne. As noted earlier, his treatise on black magic, *Daemonologie*, underscored his belief in the malevolent power of witches, influencing societal perceptions and heightening fear. The failed Gunpowder Plot of 1605, an attempt to assassinate King James and the Parliament, further fueled societal anxieties. This event, seen by many as a manifestation of demonic forces, left an indelible mark on the collective psyche, intertwining politics and supernatural fears. Shakespeare tapped into these societal tensions, using the witches to amplify the play's dramatic tension and reflect the era's unease.

On stage, the depiction of witches was a spectacle designed to captivate and unsettle. Costumes and special effects played a crucial role in creating an aura of mystery and otherworldliness. Actors donned ragged robes, their faces obscured by dark hoods, as they moved with an unnerving grace. Smoke and dim lighting enhanced the supernatural ambiance, transforming the stage into a realm of enchantment and danger. The witches' presence heightened the play's dramatic tension, their cryptic utterances and eerie demeanor captivating audiences. Their influence extended beyond the narrative, leaving a lasting impression on viewers and shaping subsequent portrayals of witchcraft in literature and media.

The legacy of Shakespeare's witches extends far beyond the confines of the Globe Theatre. Their archetypal representation has permeated literature and media, influencing countless works that explore the themes of fate and free will. Witches in later literary works often draw from Shakespeare's depiction, embodying the duality of prophecy and manipulation. Modern adaptations and interpretations continue to grapple with these themes, reflecting the enduring fascination with the mystical and the mysterious. The *weird sisters* remain a potent symbol of the unknown, their presence a reminder of the power of storytelling to capture the imagination and explore the depths of human ambition.

LITERARY DEPICTIONS OF WITCHES IN THE ENLIGHTENMENT (17TH TO EARLY 19TH CENTURY)

During the Enlightenment, a period marked by a pursuit of knowledge and reason which we will explore more in the

THE WITCH'S CHRONICLE

next chapter, writers often explored witchcraft to critique societal norms and superstitions. Voltaire's *Candide* from 1759 stands out as a masterstroke of satire. Within its pages, Voltaire uses witch trials to lampoon the absurdity of blind faith and irrational beliefs. His biting humor exposes the folly of persecuting individuals based on baseless accusations, inviting readers to question the motives and logic behind such practices. Through this lens, Voltaire encourages a shift towards rational thought, urging society to abandon fear-driven judgments.

Mary Wollstonecraft, a pioneering feminist writer, also engaged with the theme of witchcraft, albeit in a different light. Her works often highlighted the plight of women, drawing parallels between the persecution of witches and the oppression faced by women in her time. By using witchcraft as a metaphor, Wollstonecraft critiqued the patriarchal structures that confined women, advocating for equality and enlightenment. Her writings underscored the need for societal change, pushing for an era where reason and justice prevailed over superstition and inequality.

Enlightenment literature frequently juxtaposed scientific inquiry with magical thinking, promoting rationalism and skepticism. This era witnessed a growing emphasis on empirical evidence and logical reasoning, challenging the long-held beliefs in the supernatural. Writers critiqued religious and judicial authorities, exposing the flaws and abuses within systems that perpetuated witch hunts. By highlighting these contradictions, Enlightenment thinkers paved the way for a more enlightened society, one that valued critical thinking over fear and ignorance.

Key authors of the period, such as Goethe and Alexander Pope, also contributed to the discourse on witchcraft. In Goethe's *Faust*, the character of the witch serves as a vehicle for exploring themes of ambition and moral ambiguity. Faust's interaction with the witch blurs the lines between good and evil, raising questions about the nature of desire and consequence. Meanwhile, Pope's works often depicted witches in satirical contexts, using them to critique societal norms and highlight human folly.

The cultural impact of these literary depictions was profound, shifting public opinion towards a more skeptical view of witchcraft. Enlightenment literature played a crucial role in challenging the status quo, encouraging readers to question and rethink long-held beliefs. This legacy endures today, influencing modern portrayals of witches, who are now often seen as complex and multifaceted characters rather than mere embodiments of evil.

VISUAL REPRESENTATIONS: WITCHES IN ART THROUGH THE AGES

In the dimly lit corners of medieval Europe (500-1500), artists began to capture the elusive figure of the witch, a complex symbol of fear and fascination. Hans Baldung Grien's "The Witches" stands as a testament to this era's visual exploration of witchcraft. His work, filled with swirling motion and supernatural elements, captures the tension between allure and menace. Albrecht Dürer's engravings offer another perspective, with intricate details that highlight the perceived mystique and danger of witchcraft. As noted above, these pieces reflect a time when witches were viewed as both fascinating and fearsome, embodying the unknown. The art of the period serves as a visual narrative, illustrating society's ongoing struggle to understand and control the supernatural.

Moving into the Baroque period (16th century through the mid-18th century), the portrayal of witches took on a new dimension. Artists like Caravaggio utilized chiaroscuro, a technique that plays with light and shadow, to enhance the dramatic intensity of witch-themed paintings. The stark contrasts highlight the moral and metaphysical battles that defined the era. Baroque art often depicted witch trials with a theatrical flair, emphasizing the emotional turmoil and societal tensions they incited. This period's focus on drama and emotion brought an intensity to the depiction of witches, capturing the fear and fascination that surrounded them. The dramatic portrayal of witchcraft in art mirrored the heightened emotions of the time, reflecting society's continued preoccupation with the mysterious and the forbidden.

In modern art, interpretations of witches have evolved, reflecting contemporary themes and concerns. Surrealist artists, like Salvador Dalí (1904-1989), have reimagined witches through a lens of fantasy and abstraction, exploring the subconscious and challenging traditional perceptions. Feminist artists have also reclaimed the image of the witch, using it as a symbol of empowerment and rebellion against patriarchal norms. This reinterpretation highlights the ongoing struggle for gender equality and the redefinition of traditional roles. Art has become a powerful tool for challenging stereotypes and redefining the image of the witch, transforming her from a figure of fear to one of strength and defiance. Through these reinterpretations, modern art continues to explore the complexities of identity and power, offering new perspectives on an age-old symbol.

Art, with its ability to capture and convey complex ideas, has played a significant role in shaping societal views on witchcraft. The depiction of witches as symbols of rebellion, empowerment, and fear reflects broader cultural narratives. By challenging stereotypes and exploring new interpretations, art has the power to reshape perceptions and influence societal attitudes. The image of the witch, once a figure of malevolence, has become a symbol of resilience and strength, embodying the ongoing struggle for identity and autonomy.

CHAPTER 13
WITCHCRAFT IN THE AGE OF ENLIGHTENMENT

I n the bustling streets of 17th-century Europe, whispers of witchcraft mingled with the cacophony of markets and the quiet contemplation of scholars. The era, marked by the dawn of the Enlightenment, was a time when society stood at the crossroads of ancient beliefs and burgeoning scientific discovery. As the shadows of superstition lingered, the sharp light of reason began to pierce through, bringing with it a new way of understanding the world. This period, often characterized by its intellectual fervor, saw the rise of the Scientific Revolution —a movement that challenged the very foundations of previous beliefs, including the pervasive fears of witchcraft. This shift toward evidence-based reasoning marked a turning point, reshaping how people understood the natural world and their place within it.

THE SCIENTIFIC REVOLUTION AND WITCHCRAFT

The adoption of the scientific method during the Scientific Revolution played a crucial role in transforming traditional beliefs in witchcraft. This method, emphasizing observation, experimentation, and rational analysis, provided a framework for understanding phenomena that had long been shrouded in mystery. Rather than attributing misfortunes or unexplained events to witchcraft, people began to seek natural explanations grounded in empirical evidence. This shift in thinking was not just about dismissing old beliefs but about fostering a deeper understanding of the world through inquiry and skepticism.

Empiricism, which prioritized knowledge derived from sensory experience, became a cornerstone of this new approach. Figures like Francis Bacon championed the idea that careful observation and systematic experimentation could reveal truths about the natural world. This emphasis on evidence-based reasoning stood in stark contrast to the superstitions that fueled witch hunts. As natural philosophy emerged as a discipline, it brought with it the tools necessary to question and ultimately debunk the myths that had long held sway over society.

Notable scientists of the time played pivotal roles in challenging and reshaping these perceptions. Sir Isaac Newton, renowned for his groundbreaking work in physics, used his laws of motion to explain natural phenomena in ways that were previously unimaginable. Newton's approach to science, grounded in mathematical rigor and empirical observation, provided a model for understanding the universe without recourse to supernatural explanations. His work demonstrated that the laws governing the cosmos were consistent and predictable, undermining the notion that witches could manipulate the natural world through magic. Newton's disbelief in demons as literal entities, as revealed in his unpublished manuscripts, further exemplified his commitment to rational thought over superstition.

Robert Boyle, another key figure in the Scientific Revolution, conducted experiments that shifted the focus from mystical explanations to ones rooted in natural law. Boyle's work in chemistry, particularly his experiments on gases, showed that seemingly mysterious changes in matter could be understood through scientific inquiry. He promoted the idea that natural phenomena were governed by physical principles rather than supernatural forces, influencing how people viewed the world.

Johannes Kepler, known for his contributions to astronomy, also expressed skepticism about witch trials. His understanding of planetary motion and celestial mechanics highlighted the predictability and order of the universe, challenging the chaotic and malevolent forces attributed to witchcraft.

Scientific societies and academies played a crucial role in disseminating these new ideas. The Royal Society, founded in 1660, became a hub for scientific inquiry and innovation. Through public lectures and publications, the Society promoted rationalism and skepticism, encouraging the examination of traditional beliefs with a critical eye. These efforts helped to spread the principles of the scientific method, fostering a culture of inquiry that valued evidence over superstition.

As scientific thinking gained traction, witch trials began to decline. The correlation between the rise of scientific reasoning and the reduction in witchcraft prosecutions is evident in the gradual repeal of witchcraft laws across Europe. The crime of witchcraft was abolished in France in 1682, repealed in England in 1736, and in Poland in 1776. This shift marked a move towards legal reforms that emphasized the need for tangible evidence in court proceedings. As the reliance on supernatural explanations waned among the elite, the rigorous application of scientific reasoning in legal contexts made it increasingly difficult to justify witchcraft accusations.

ENLIGHTENMENT THINKERS AND THE DEMYSTIFICATION OF WITCHES

In the vibrant salons and dimly lit studies of 18th-century Europe, a new wave of thinking began to reshape society. The Enlightenment, often referred to as the Age of Reason, ignited a philosophical shift toward rationalism that challenged long-held beliefs, including the fear of witchcraft. This intellectual movement was characterized by a profound belief in the power of human reason to understand and improve the world. Philosophers of the Enlightenment advocated for critical thinking and skepticism, urging individuals to question traditional authority and dogma that had long gone unchallenged. This new emphasis on reason became a guiding principle, encouraging a departure from superstition and mysticism that had fueled witch hunts for centuries.

Among the prominent figures of the Enlightenment, Voltaire stood out as a vocal critic of superstition and fanaticism. Known for his wit and sharp intellect, Voltaire used his writings to ridicule practices he saw as irrational, including the persecution of witches. In his many works, he highlighted the absurdity of witch trials, portraying them as relics of a less enlightened time. Through satire, Voltaire encouraged his readers to embrace reason and humanity over fear and ignorance, contributing to the gradual decline of witch hunts. His belief in the power of reason to dismantle superstition resonated deeply, inspiring others to question the validity of witchcraft accusations.

Montesquieu, another influential thinker, contributed to this shift through his writings on the separation of powers and legal reform. His seminal work, "The Spirit of the Laws," argued for a government structure that would prevent the abuse of power, promoting a legal system based on reason and justice rather than fear and superstition. Montesquieu's ideas laid the groundwork for modern legal frameworks, advocating for fairness and due process in judicial proceedings. By emphasizing rational principles, he helped pave the way for the reform of laws that had once legitimized witch trials, ensuring that justice was grounded in evidence rather than hysteria.

Denis Diderot played a crucial role in compiling the "Encyclopédie," an ambitious project aimed at gathering and disseminating human knowledge. As a source of rational thought, the "Encyclopédie" challenged traditional beliefs, including those surrounding witchcraft. By compiling articles that emphasized scientific and philosophical understanding, Diderot and his collaborators sought to educate the public and promote critical thinking. This monumental work became an emblem of the Enlightenment, symbolizing the shift from superstition to reason. It provided a platform for discussing and debunking myths, encouraging society to embrace a more rational worldview.

Enlightenment literature also played a significant role in reshaping public perceptions of witches. Writers used satire and irony to critique the irrationality of witch hunts, exposing the flaws and injustices inherent in such practices. These literary works often portrayed witches as misunderstood individuals rather than malevolent beings, challenging the stereotypes that had long dehumanized them. Through stories and essays, Enlightenment authors encouraged readers to see witches as victims of societal fear rather than perpetrators of evil. This shift in portrayal helped to humanize those accused of witchcraft, fostering empathy and understanding where there had once been suspicion and fear.

The legacy of Enlightenment thought on the perception of witchcraft is profound and lasting. As Enlightenment ideas spread throughout Europe, societies began to shift toward secularism, gradually moving away from the religious and superstitious beliefs that had dominated for centuries. This transition marked a significant cultural shift, as reason and empirical evidence became the foundations for understanding the world. The influence of Enlightenment principles extended beyond philosophy, shaping modern legal and educational systems. Laws once rooted in fear and superstition were reformed to reflect principles of justice and rationality, ensuring that future generations would inherit a more enlightened society.

In summary, the Enlightenment marked a pivotal moment in the history of witchcraft, as reason and critical thinking challenged and ultimately transformed societal perceptions. The contributions of Enlightenment thinkers and writers left an indelible mark, paving the way for a world where reason triumphed over superstition. As we move forward, the lessons of the Enlightenment continue to resonate, reminding us of the power of reason to illuminate the darkest corners of human belief.

CHAPTER 14

THE EVOLUTION OF WITCHCRAFT PERCEPTIONS

THE ROMANTICIZATION OF WITCHES IN THE 19TH CENTURY

I n the 19th century, the figure of the witch began to emerge from the shadows of fear and superstition, her image transformed by the era's artistic and literary imagination. This period, characterized by its fascination with the mysterious and the supernatural, saw witches reimagined not as malevolent hags, but as enigmatic figures worthy of intrigue and allure. As you delve into this chapter, you'll discover how the cultural narratives of the time shifted to portray witches in a more romantic and mystical light, reflecting broader societal changes and the evolution of artistic expression.

The 19th century's Gothic literature played a pivotal role in reshaping the themes associated with witchcraft. Emerging in the late 18th century, the Gothic movement captivated audiences with its exploration of the macabre and the unknown. It introduced elements of horror, mystery, and the supernatural, creating a fertile ground for the witch to be reimagined. In this genre, witches were no longer one-dimensional villains but complex characters with depth and nuance. The Gothic tale's emphasis on atmosphere and emotion provided the perfect backdrop for the witch's transformation, allowing her to step into the realm of the sublime. This period marked a departure from strictly moralistic depictions, opening the door for more nuanced portrayals that embraced ambiguity.

Romantic poets also contributed significantly to the evolution of the witch's image. Figures such as John Keats infused their work with a sense of longing and melancholy, imbuing witches with a tragic beauty. In Keats' poem "La Belle Dame sans Merci," the bewitching woman lures the knight with her ethereal charm, embodying both enchantment and danger. This duality captured the Romantic fascination with the tension between the natural and the supernatural, highlighting the witch's allure as both muse and menace. The Romantic movement's focus on emotion and individual experience allowed poets to explore the witch as a symbol of untamed nature and the human psyche's darker recesses, enriching her character with layers of complexity.

Literature from the era further solidified the romanticization of witches through key works and authors. "The Witch of Edmonton," a play by Thomas Dekker, William Rowley, and John Ford, presents a sympathetic portrayal of a witch, challenging contemporary views of witchcraft as inherently evil. The play's exploration of societal pressures and individual suffering reflects a growing awareness of the witch as a figure shaped by her circumstances. Nathaniel Hawthorne's "The Scarlet Letter" also delves into themes of sin, redemption, and societal judgment, with witchcraft woven into its narrative as a symbol of rebellion against oppressive norms. These works, along with others, expanded the literary landscape, inviting readers to question and reconsider the simplistic archetypes that had long defined witches.

Folklore and fairy tales of the 19th century further contributed to the evolving perception of witches. The Brothers Grimm, with their collection of tales, solidified the witch's place in cultural memory, blending familiar motifs with a sense of wonder and fear. Their stories, although steeped in tradition, allowed for new interpretations, presenting witches as both antagonists and wise figures. Victorian fairy tales continued this trend, using witch motifs to explore themes of transformation and redemption. These tales, with their imaginative narratives, engaged audiences in a dialogue about the nature of good and evil, encouraging a more nuanced understanding of witches and their role in the human experience.

The romanticization of witches during this period also reflected broader societal changes and attitudes toward women and the supernatural. The 19th century was marked by a burgeoning interest in spiritualism and the occult, as people sought to connect with the mystical and the transcendent. This interest paralleled advances in psychology, as thinkers began to explore the unconscious mind and its mysteries. Witches, embodying both the spiritual and the psychological, became symbols of the unknown forces at play within and beyond the human experience. This intersection of spiritualism and psychology contributed to the witch's allure, positioning her as a figure who defied easy categorization.

Societal changes during this time influenced the way witches were perceived, particularly in relation to gender. As the role of women in society began to shift, the witch emerged as a symbol of both empowerment and fear. Her defiance of traditional norms resonated with those who sought to challenge societal constraints, while her association with the supernatural tapped into deep-seated anxieties about female autonomy. The romanticization of witches mirrored the complexities of these changing attitudes, offering a space for exploring the tensions between power, freedom, and fear.

MODERN WITCHCRAFT MOVEMENTS AND FEMINISM

In the midst of the 20th century, a transformative period for witchcraft began. This era saw the emergence of modern witchcraft movements, which intertwined with burgeoning feminist ideologies. At the forefront of this revival was the founding of Wicca by Gerald Gardner in the mid-20th century. Gardner, a retired British civil servant,

introduced Wicca as a contemporary pagan religious movement, blending ancient practices with modern interpretations. He presented Wicca as a structured belief system that
emphasized harmony with nature and personal empowerment. This new form of witchcraft provided a spiritual
framework that resonated with many seeking alternatives
to traditional religious paths. Wicca offered rituals, celebrations of natural cycles, and a pantheon that included both
male and female deities, reflecting a balance of gender that
was particularly appealing to those disillusioned with
patriarchal religious structures.

The rise of Wicca coincided with the waves of feminism
that swept through the latter half of the 20th century.
Second-wave feminism, which focused on issues such as
equality, reproductive rights, and challenging gender roles,
found a natural ally in the symbolism and ethos of witchcraft. Witches, historically marginalized and vilified,
became powerful symbols of resistance against patriarchal
oppression. The feminist movement embraced this
imagery, reclaiming the witch as a figure of empowerment
and autonomy. Witchcraft, with its roots in defiance and its
rejection of societal norms, became a potent emblem of
feminist resistance and renewal. This reclamation was not
just symbolic; it reflected a deeper alignment of values, as
both movements sought to challenge and dismantle structures of power that limited individual freedom and
expression.

Witchcraft's role in feminist discourse expanded as
activists and thinkers began to explore its potential as a

tool for social change. The publication of Arthur Evans's "Witchcraft and the Gay Counterculture" in the 1970s highlighted the intersections between witchcraft, feminism, and LGBTQ+ liberation. Evans's work emphasized how witchcraft and paganism offered alternative spiritual paths that celebrated diversity and challenged conventional norms. This perspective resonated with many who sought to break free from rigid societal expectations. Witchcraft's symbols and rituals were incorporated into feminist protests and movements, serving both as a means of empowerment and as a form of protest against systemic injustices. The image of the witch, historically persecuted yet resilient, inspired those fighting for equality and recognition.

Key figures and organizations have played significant roles in promoting modern witchcraft and feminist ideals. Starhawk, an influential voice in eco-feminist spirituality, published "The Spiral Dance" in 1979, a seminal work that combined feminist theory with pagan rituals. Her teachings emphasized the interconnectedness of all life and the importance of ecological balance, aligning closely with feminist principles of equality and justice. The Reclaiming Collective, co-founded by Starhawk, further advanced these ideas, promoting a form of witchcraft that was both spiritually fulfilling and politically active. This collective sought to empower individuals through education, community building, and activism, fostering a space where spirituality and social justice could coexist and flourish.

Modern witchcraft movements have also significantly

impacted popular culture, influencing how witches are portrayed in media and public discourse. Television shows like "Buffy the Vampire Slayer" and "Charmed" brought witchcraft into the mainstream, presenting witches as complex characters with agency and depth. These portrayals challenged traditional stereotypes, offering narratives where witches were heroes rather than villains. The rise of social media has further amplified witchcraft's visibility, with online communities and influencers sharing practices, rituals, and personal experiences. Platforms like Instagram and TikTok have become spaces for modern witches to connect, share insights, and build supportive networks, contributing to a vibrant and diverse global witchcraft community.

The globalization of modern witchcraft movements has been facilitated by the internet, allowing practices and beliefs to spread across cultural and geographic boundaries. This exchange has led to the adaptation and integration of witchcraft practices in non-Western contexts, enriching the global tapestry of spiritual traditions. The internet has played a pivotal role in connecting practitioners worldwide, fostering a sense of community and shared purpose. This connectivity has allowed for the cross-pollination of ideas, leading to innovative practices that reflect the diverse backgrounds of those who identify with witchcraft. As witchcraft continues to evolve and expand, it remains a dynamic and inclusive movement, embracing change while honoring its roots.

This chapter has explored the profound shifts in witchcraft perceptions over the centuries, highlighting its resurgence as a force for empowerment and social change. As we move forward, we will delve into how witchcraft has been preserved and celebrated as a cultural heritage, examining its impact on modern identity and community.

CHAPTER 15
WITCHCRAFT AND CULTURAL IDENTITY

WITCHCRAFT IN HISPANIC AND LATIN AMERICA CULTURES

I n the vibrant streets of Havana, where the air pulses with the rhythm of salsa and the scent of cigars, a different kind of energy weaves through the crowd—a spiritual tapestry that connects the living with the divine. Here, in the heart of Cuba, Santería thrives, a syncretic religion that marries the African Yoruba faith with Catholicism. It is a testament to the resilience and adaptability of cultural belief systems, born from necessity during the colonial era when enslaved Africans were forced to mask their spiritual practices under the guise of Catholic rituals. Santería's orishas, or deities, align with Catholic saints, allowing practitioners to honor their ancestors and maintain a connection with their heritage despite oppressive circumstances. This blend of traditions speaks to the enduring power of cultural identity, providing a spiritual anchor in turbulent times.

As you journey further into Latin America, you encounter a kaleidoscope of witchcraft practices, each reflecting the unique history and culture of its people. In Mexico, curanderismo stands as a cornerstone of traditional healing, a rich blend of indigenous, Catholic, and African influences. Curanderos and curanderas, the healers within this tradition, offer holistic healing that addresses the physical, spiritual, and mental aspects of well-being. Known for their extensive knowledge of herbs and cultural remedies, curanderos work within their communities, offering spiritual cleansing and guidance alongside conventional medical treatments when necessary. Their role extends beyond mere physical healing; they serve as spiritual counselors, helping individuals navigate life's challenges and traumas. This practice, rooted in compassion and community, underscores the deep connection between health and spirituality in Mexican culture.

The Caribbean, with its vibrant mix of cultures, hosts its own unique expressions of witchcraft. Brujería, a practice often misunderstood, holds cultural significance across the islands. It represents a fusion of indigenous Taíno, African, and European elements, reflecting the region's complex colonial history. Brujería is not monolithic; it varies from island to island, adapting to the local customs and beliefs. In some places, it is seen as a form of resistance, a way to reclaim power and assert cultural identity in the face of colonial oppression. Shamans in the Andean regions of

South America further illustrate the diversity of witchcraft practices. These spiritual leaders maintain a close relationship with the land, drawing on ancient knowledge to perform rituals that honor the earth and its cycles. Their practices are deeply rooted in the cosmology of the Andean people, emphasizing harmony between humans and nature.

Colonialism left an indelible mark on these practices, shaping them into forms of cultural resistance. In Peru and Bolivia, indigenous communities have long used witchcraft to preserve their cultural identity and resist colonial pressures. Even as colonial powers sought to suppress indigenous beliefs, these communities found ways to adapt and continue their traditions, often in secret. Witchcraft became a symbol of resilience, a way to maintain a connection to their ancestral roots. In the Caribbean, enslaved Africans used witchcraft as a tool of resistance, employing it in slave rebellions and uprisings against their oppressors. These practices, rooted in African traditions, provided hope and empowerment, uniting communities in their struggle for freedom.

Today, the legacy of these practices continues to evolve, reflecting the changing dynamics of modern society. In Mexico, a resurgence of interest in traditional witchcraft among young people has sparked a cultural revival. This renewed interest is driven by a desire to reconnect with heritage and explore alternative spiritual paths. Witchcraft provides a means of empowerment and self-expression, offering a counter-narrative to mainstream culture. Moreover, the global reach of media has brought Latin American witchcraft into the spotlight, influencing popular culture and inspiring new interpretations. Music, film, and literature have embraced these themes, contributing to a broader appreciation and understanding of these rich cultural traditions.

ASIAN WITCHCRAFT TRADITIONS AND THEIR LEGACY

In the heart of Korea, a tradition as old as the mountains unfolds, one that bridges the earthly with the ethereal. Korean shamanism, known as Mudang, is a practice where shamans, predominantly women, serve as intermediaries between the human world and the spirits. These shamans, or mudang, perform rituals that include divination and the kut, a ceremony aimed at appeasing spirits and seeking guidance. These practices are deeply embedded in Korean culture, reflecting a belief system that acknowledges the influence of spirits in daily life. The mudang are not merely spiritual guides; they are integral to the social fabric, providing counsel in matters ranging from health to happiness. This role emphasizes the importance of spiritual balance and harmony in Korean communities, where the intersection of the earthly and the spiritual is a daily reality.

Moving eastward to China, the realm of Taoist magic and alchemy reveals a different facet of Asian witchcraft. Rooted in the ancient philosophy of Taoism, these practices emphasize harmony with the Tao, or the fundamental nature of the universe. Taoist magicians and alchemists seek to achieve immortality and enlightenment through a deep understanding of the natural world and its energies. Their rituals often involve complex processes, including the creation of elixirs and the use of talismans, each symbolizing an aspect of the practitioner's spiritual journey. Alchemy, in particular, represents a quest for transformation, where the practitioner seeks not only physical longevity but also spiritual elevation. This pursuit of harmony and balance is central to Taoist practices, echoing the broader philosophical tenets of Taoism itself.

In Southeast Asia, the rich tapestry of Hindu and Buddhist influences weaves through local witchcraft practices. Here, rituals are often seen as extensions of religious beliefs, with a focus on achieving spiritual purity and enlightenment. Hindu epics like the Ramayana and Mahabharata provide narratives where magic and witchcraft play pivotal roles. These stories, deeply ingrained in cultural consciousness, present characters who wield supernatural powers, reflecting the complex interplay between human frailty and divine intervention. In Buddhist traditions, rituals often emphasize mindfulness and the cessation of suffering, with witchcraft serving as a metaphor for overcoming ignorance and desire. The integration of these religious elements into local practices highlights the adaptability and resilience of witchcraft in the region, where it continues to thrive as a vibrant and evolving tradition.

Japanese Shintoism offers another unique perspective

on the integration of witchcraft and religion. Shinto, a belief system rooted in animism, acknowledges the presence of kami, or spirits, in all aspects of the natural world. This animistic worldview allows for the seamless incorporation of witchcraft practices, viewed as a means of communicating with and influencing these spirits. In Shinto ceremonies, rituals are performed to honor the kami, seeking their favor and guidance for a harmonious existence. These practices emphasize the interconnectedness of all living things, reflecting a deep respect for nature and its mysteries. The role of witchcraft in Shintoism illustrates the fluid boundaries between religion and magic in Japanese culture, where the sacred and the supernatural coexist in harmony.

The societal perception of witch doctors, such as the "Bomoh" in Malaysia, underscores their vital role in community health. The Bomoh combines spiritual rituals with herbal remedies to address ailments, drawing from extensive knowledge of local flora and fauna. This holistic practice, which integrates Islamic and Hindu beliefs, has been passed down through generations, emphasizing the interconnectedness of body, mind, and spirit. Despite the rise of Western medicine, the Bomoh remains a trusted figure, particularly in rural areas where access to modern healthcare is limited. Their ability to offer both physical and spiritual healing makes them indispensable, bridging the gap between tradition and modernity.

Similarly, in the Philippines, the Albularyo serves as a community healer, blending spiritual and herbal remedies to treat a wide range of ailments. The Albularyo's practice is deeply rooted in Filipino culture, where the belief in spirits and the supernatural plays a significant role in daily life. These practitioners are often the first point of contact for individuals seeking relief from illness, offering treatments that address both the symptoms and the underlying spiritual imbalances. The Albularyo embodies the cultural synthesis of indigenous, Catholic, and Western influences, reflecting the dynamic nature of Filipino healing traditions.

Colonial encounters significantly impacted the practices and perceptions of witch doctors in Eastern cultures. In India, the arrival of Western medicine during colonial rule disrupted traditional healing practices, such as Ayurveda. Colonial narratives often portrayed these practitioners as primitive or exotic, undermining their legitimacy and marginalizing their practices. This perception was reflected in the introduction of legislation to regulate traditional medicine, which sought to impose Western standards of treatment and dismiss indigenous knowledge as mere superstition. However, traditional practices proved resilient, adapting to new influences while preserving their core philosophies.

Modern challenges for witch doctors include navigating the tensions between traditional practices and contemporary healthcare systems. Globalization and technological advancements have introduced new methods and ideas, leading to a reevaluation of indigenous practices. Efforts to revitalize traditional healing are underway, with communities and practitioners working to preserve these cultural traditions for future generations. Initiatives include documenting traditional knowledge, integrating it with modern healthcare, and promoting its value through education and cultural exchange. These efforts highlight the enduring relevance of witch doctors, whose practices continue to offer insights into holistic health and cultural identity.

Historically, witchcraft in Asia has undergone significant transformations, shaped by both internal dynamics and external pressures. During the Joseon Dynasty in Korea, witchcraft persecutions were not uncommon. The state, influenced by Confucian ideals, viewed shamanistic practices with suspicion, often equating them with superstition and disorder. Despite these challenges, shamanism persisted, adapting to changing times and continuing to play a vital role in Korean culture. In post-colonial Southeast Asia, there has been a revival of spiritual practices, as communities seek to reclaim their cultural heritage and resist the homogenizing forces of globalization. This revival underscores the enduring significance of witchcraft in the region, where it continues to be a source of identity and resilience.

In modern Asian societies, witchcraft remains a powerful symbol of cultural identity and heritage. It serves as a reminder of the rich traditions that have shaped communities across the continent, offering a link to the past and a source of inspiration for the future. For many, these practices are not merely relics of history but living traditions that continue to evolve and adapt. They provide a framework for understanding the world and one's place within it, emphasizing the importance of balance, harmony, and respect for the unseen forces that govern life. As we explore these traditions, we gain insight into the diverse ways in which human societies have engaged with the mystical, reflecting the universal quest for meaning and connection.

This exploration of Asian witchcraft traditions reveals a rich tapestry of beliefs and practices, each contributing to the cultural identity and heritage of their respective societies. As we move forward, we will examine how these traditions intersect with contemporary issues and continue to influence the modern world.

WITCHCRAFT IN AUSTRALIAN ABORIGINAL CULTURES

In the vast and ancient landscapes of Australia, where the red earth stretches to meet the endless sky, Aboriginal cultures have long woven their lives with the spiritual narratives known as the Dreamtime. These stories, passed down through generations, form the bedrock of Aboriginal identity, explaining the creation of the world and the interconnectedness of all beings. Within this rich tapestry, witchcraft holds a unique place, deeply intertwined with the Dreamtime and cultural practices that govern daily life. Central to these practices is the concept of the *kurdaitcha*, a term that denotes a traditional healer or executioner, often called upon to maintain justice and balance within the community. The *kurdaitcha* is a figure of both reverence and fear, tasked with carrying out punishments for serious transgressions through ritual means. Their role is not merely punitive but is seen as essential to upholding the moral and spiritual fabric of the community.

Songlines, or dreaming tracks, are another crucial element of Aboriginal spirituality, serving as both maps and narratives that guide the people across the land. These songlines are imbued with the spirits of ancestors and are used to navigate the vast terrains, linking sacred sites and telling the stories of creation. They are not just paths but living manifestations of the Dreamtime, connecting the physical and spiritual worlds. Sacred sites along these songlines hold immense power, often serving as places of ceremony and healing where the spiritual and the material meet. The use of these sites in rituals underscores the deep relationship between the land and the Aboriginal people, where every feature of the landscape has significance and meaning.

Aboriginal witchcraft practices are marked by unique traditions that reflect the cultural significance of spirituality and justice. One such practice is "pointing the bone," a form of curse or retribution that involves the use of a bone to direct harmful intentions toward an individual. This act is believed to be so powerful that it can cause illness or even death, not through physical means but through the psychological impact on the victim, who believes in the curse's efficacy. The practice highlights the profound influence of belief and community consensus in Aboriginal cultures, where the fear of spiritual retribution reinforces social norms and cohesion.

Totems and ancestral spirits play a vital role in Aboriginal witchcraft, serving as sources of identity, protection, and healing. Each individual is associated with a totem, which connects them to a specific animal or natural element, linking them to the broader ecosystem and their ancestors. These totems guide behavior, inform relationships, and provide spiritual support, embodying the principles of balance and harmony central to Aboriginal life. Ancestral spirits are also invoked in healing practices, called upon to restore health and well-being by realigning the individual's spiritual essence with the natural world.

The arrival of European settlers brought profound changes and challenges to Aboriginal witchcraft practices. Colonial authorities, often misunderstanding or fearing these traditions, sought to suppress them through policies of assimilation and displacement. Traditional practices were stigmatized, leading to a loss of cultural knowledge as communities were forced to abandon their lands and adapt to new ways of life. These policies aimed to erase Aboriginal identity, viewing it as incompatible with Western ideals of progress and civilization. The impact of colonization was devastating, disrupting the transmission of cultural knowledge and severing the connection to the land, which is fundamental to Aboriginal spirituality.

In response to these challenges, contemporary efforts to preserve and revitalize Aboriginal witchcraft traditions have gained momentum. Aboriginal elders play a crucial role in passing down traditional knowledge, ensuring that the stories, songs, and practices of the past continue to guide future generations. Cultural festivals and exhibitions have emerged as vital platforms for celebrating Aboriginal spirituality, providing opportunities for education and community engagement. These events, often held at sacred sites, allow for the sharing of cultural narratives and foster a sense of pride and identity among Aboriginal peoples. Additionally, there is a growing movement to integrate traditional practices into modern healing and community-building efforts, recognizing their value in promoting well-being and resilience.

By embracing these traditions, Aboriginal communities are reclaiming their cultural heritage and reinforcing their connection to the land. These efforts underscore the enduring power of Aboriginal spirituality and its relevance in contemporary society, offering insights into the universal quest for meaning and connection with the natural world. As we move forward, it is vital to acknowledge and respect these rich cultural traditions, recognizing their significance not only for Aboriginal peoples but for the broader tapestry of human experience.

CHAPTER 16
PERSONAL ACCOUNTS AND HUMAN STORIES

TESTIMONIES FROM THE ACCUSED: VOICES FROM
THE PAST

I n the dim glow of a flickering candle, Isobel Gowdie
sat, her heart pounding against her ribs. She spoke of
magic, not as a distant fantasy, but as a palpable
force that coursed through her life in 17th-century Scotland.
Her confessions, delivered over six haunting weeks, have
become some of the most detailed records of witchcraft
beliefs from that era. Isobel professed allegiance to a coven
serving the Devil, describing vivid encounters with the fairy
queen and king. Her tales, rich with details of shapeshifting
and magical arrows, paint a vivid picture of a world where
the mystical and the mundane intertwined. Some scholars
speculate that Isobel's vivid imagination may have been
fueled by ergotism, a condition that could induce halluci-

nations. Yet, her words have endured, offering a window into the beliefs and fears that gripped her society.

Across the ocean, in the tight-knit community of Salem, Massachusetts, Rebecca Nurse faced her accusers with unwavering dignity. Despite her age and respected status, she found herself ensnared in the hysteria of the Salem Witch Trials. The accusations against her, spearheaded by the Putnam family, seemed to stem from long-standing land disputes rather than genuine belief in her guilt. During her trial, Rebecca maintained her innocence, her calm demeanor starkly contrasting with the chaos around her. Initially found not guilty, the verdict was cruelly reversed, leading to her execution. Her death marked a turning point, sowing seeds of doubt about the legitimacy of the trials and forcing a community to confront its own injustices.

Meanwhile, in the shadows of the Holy Roman Empire, Katharina Kepler endured a grueling six-year ordeal. Accused of witchcraft, she faced allegations of poisoning and maleficium from her neighbors. Her son, Johannes Kepler, a renowned astronomer, abandoned his celestial studies to defend her. His defense was a masterclass in rhetoric, weaving scientific reasoning with heartfelt appeals. Katharina, chained in a cell, faced the specter of torture. Her resilience in the face of such adversity is remarkable. Eventually, Johannes succeeded in securing her release, yet the trial left indelible marks on their lives, illustrating the precarious balance between superstition and emerging scientific thought.

The Pendle Witch Trials in England offer another poignant glimpse into the human cost of witchcraft accusations. Alice Nutter, unlike many of her co-accused, hailed from a noble background. Her wealth and status, rather than shielding her, may have heightened suspicions. Accused by a child, Jennet Device, Alice was denied the right to call witnesses in her defense. Her letters, written during her imprisonment, reveal a woman steadfast in her innocence, yet resigned to her fate. Executed alongside other accused witches, Alice's story highlights the tragic intersection of wealth, power, and fear in a society eager to purge itself of perceived threats.

These testimonies, drawn from various corners of history, reveal the emotional and psychological toll exacted on those accused of witchcraft. Isolation was a common thread, as communities turned their backs on individuals once loved and respected. Accusations often led to ostracization, creating a chasm between the accused and their former lives. Fear and anxiety permeated their existence, the threat of execution looming like a dark cloud. Yet, within this darkness, there were glimmers of defiance. Some, like Katharina, refused to confess, even under the threat of torture, clinging to their truth as a beacon of hope.

The diversity of experiences among the accused is striking. Elderly women, like Rebecca Nurse, faced unique challenges, their age and frailty juxtaposing the vigor with which they defended their innocence. Children, too, were not immune, often caught in the crossfire of adult rivalries and fears. Their testimonies, sometimes coerced, added layers of complexity to the trials. Social standing played a crucial role; those with influence, like Alice Nutter, found themselves navigating treacherous waters, where wealth was both an asset and a liability.

The documentation of these trials has profoundly influenced historical interpretation and public memory. Court scribes meticulously recorded testimonies, yet their writings were shaped by the biases and pressures of their time. Pamphlets and publications, consumed by a curious public, often sensationalized events, blurring the line between fact and fiction. Distinguishing coerced confessions from genuine testimony remains a challenge, as historians sift through layers of narrative to uncover the truths within. These records, while imperfect, serve as poignant reminders of the human stories at the heart of witch hunts, inviting reflection on the enduring impact of fear and the resilience of the human spirit.

THE IMPACT OF WITCHCRAFT ACCUSATIONS ON FAMILIES

In the dimly lit chambers of the past, where fear cast long shadows, the reverberations of witchcraft accusations extended far beyond the accused individuals themselves. Families found themselves ensnared in a web of suspicion and resentment. The repercussions were swift and severe, often leading to the confiscation of family property and wealth. Authorities seized lands and possessions, leaving families destitute. This loss of economic stability wasn't just a financial blow—it was a social one. In tightly-knit communities, where reputation was as valuable as coin, the stigma of witchcraft left deep scars. Once respected families became pariahs, shunned and whispered about, their social standing obliterated overnight.

For many families, the struggle for survival became an all-consuming reality. With breadwinners imprisoned or executed, the remaining family members faced the harsh task of maintaining livelihoods in hostile environments. Children, robbed of their childhood innocence, were often forced to step into adult roles, working tirelessly to keep their families afloat. The fear of further accusations loomed large, creating an atmosphere of distrust and paranoia. Every interaction was tinged with caution, every glance scrutinized for hidden malice. Families were torn apart, not just by the physical absence of loved ones but by the emotional void left in their wake.

The emotional and psychological toll on these families, particularly on the children, was profound. Young ones, who once found comfort in their parents' arms, witnessed the terrifying spectacle of arrests and trials. The sight of a parent being led away, framed by the harsh cries of accusers, etched itself into their memories, leaving indelible marks of fear and trauma. These children often experienced a sense of displacement, forced to navigate a world that suddenly seemed unpredictable and cruel. The fear of accusation became a specter, haunting their dreams and shaping their interactions with others. Some lived in constant worry, their lives overshadowed by the dread that they, too, could fall victim to the same fate that befell their kin.

Yet, amidst the despair, stories of resilience and solidarity emerged. Families, despite the odds, banded together to support their accused loved ones. Acts of defiance, such as gathering evidence or seeking testimonies to prove innocence, became acts of resistance against an oppressive system. Community networks sometimes offered refuge, providing safe havens and moral support, defying societal pressures to abandon those deemed guilty. Petitions for clemency, though often unsuccessful, were brave attempts to sway the hearts of those in power, testaments to the enduring bonds of familial love and loyalty.

The long-term impact of these accusations reverberated through family legacies and historical memory. The stories of accused ancestors, passed down through generations, became cautionary tales woven into the fabric of family history. These narratives shaped family identities, influencing how descendants viewed their past and their place within it. Genealogical research often unearthed these stories, prompting reflection on the enduring effects of historical injustices. In some cases, families sought public recognition of their ancestors' suffering, participating in commemorative efforts to honor and remember those who endured persecution. These initiatives aimed to restore dignity to tarnished names, providing a sense of closure and justice long denied.

This chapter, with its focus on the familial impact of witchcraft accusations, highlights the broader societal implications of fear and superstition. As we move forward, the next chapter will explore the legal reforms and societal shifts that eventually ended witch trials, setting the stage for a world striving for justice and reason.

CHAPTER 17
LEGAL AND SOCIAL REFORMS

In the dim light of an 18th-century courtroom, a scene unfolds that would signal a monumental shift in legal history. The air is tense with anticipation as the accused, Jane Wenham, stands trial for witchcraft. This trial wasn't just another chapter in the saga of persecution; it was a turning point. The case of Jane Wenham, a widow from Walkern, Hertfordshire, accused of casting spells on a servant, drew significant attention. As villagers testified against her, the presiding judge, John Powell, questioned the validity of the evidence presented. His skepticism marked a departure from the blind acceptance of accusations that had characterized previous witch trials. The outcome was revolutionary—Wenham was acquitted, setting a precedent for the decline of witchcraft prosecutions in England. This moment symbolized a broader transformation in legal standards and judicial practices, reflecting a society on the cusp of enlightenment.

LEGAL REFORM: THE END OF WITCH TRIALS

The Wenham trial was part of a broader movement across Europe to reform the legal approach to witchcraft. As the Enlightenment dawned, empirical reason began to challenge the superstitions that had fueled witch hunts for centuries. Legal systems started to demand tangible evidence rather than relying on spectral evidence, which was based on dreams, visions, or intangible claims. This shift was crucial in dismantling the judicial mechanisms that had sustained witch trials. In many European countries, laws were revised to abolish witchcraft as a criminal offense, reflecting a growing recognition of the need for justice grounded in reason and evidence.

The Enlightenment's influence on legal reforms was profound. Thinkers like Montesquieu, with his theory of the separation of powers, advocated for a legal system where checks and balances would prevent abuses of power. Montesquieu's ideas, articulated in works like "The Spirit of the Laws," argued for a government structure that could safeguard individual liberties. This philosophy resonated deeply within legal circles, prompting a reevaluation of judicial practices and the role of evidence in court proceedings. At the same time, Voltaire emerged as a vocal critic of judicial abuses, including those evident in witch trials. His writings highlighted the irrationality and injustice of using torture to extract confessions, advocating for reforms that aligned with principles of fairness and humanity.

Landmark cases during this period further cemented the shift away from witch trials. In Salem, Massachusetts, where the hysteria of 1692 had led to the execution of 19 individuals, a reversal of convictions and pardoning of the accused took place in the years that followed. This act served as a public acknowledgment of the miscarriages of justice that had occurred and underscored the necessity of legal reform. Similarly, Jane Wenham's acquittal in England symbolized a broader societal shift towards skepticism and rationality in the face of unfounded accusations.

Prominent individuals and groups played critical roles in advocating for these legal reforms. Intellectuals, reformers, and even some religious leaders began to question the morality and efficacy of witch trials. Their efforts were instrumental in fostering an environment where reason and evidence took precedence over fear and superstition. These advocates worked tirelessly to challenge the status quo, often facing resistance from those who clung to traditional beliefs. Their legacy is a testament to the power of reason and the enduring impact of the Enlightenment on modern legal systems.

As we consider the impact of these reforms, it's essential to reflect on the broader societal and cultural shifts they represent. The decline of witch trials marked a critical juncture in the evolution of justice, where legal systems began to prioritize individual rights and evidence-based decision-making. This transformation laid the groundwork for the development of modern legal standards and practices, emphasizing the importance of fairness, due process, and the protection of civil liberties. The journey from superstition to reason was neither quick nor easy, but it was a vital step towards a more just and equitable society.

SOCIAL CHANGE AND WITCHCRAFT ACCEPTANCE

As the world moved beyond the Age of Enlightenment and into the Romantic era, cultural and societal shifts began to transform how witchcraft was perceived. Romanticism, with its emphasis on emotion, nature, and the sublime, played a pivotal role in reshaping views of the supernatural. This movement encouraged a fascination with mystery and enchantment, and people started to view witches not as malevolent figures but as symbols of untamed nature and human emotion. Art and literature of the time often depicted witches as misunderstood beings, aligning them with the Romantic ideal of the misunderstood genius or the noble outcast. This shift laid the groundwork for a more nuanced understanding of witchcraft, moving it from the realm of fear into one of fascination.

The 20th century witnessed another significant transformation in the perception of witchcraft, driven largely by the counterculture movement. This era, characterized by a questioning of authority and a search for alternative spiritual paths, provided fertile ground for the acceptance of witchcraft as a legitimate spiritual practice. The counterculture movement, with its emphasis on personal liberation and communal living, embraced diverse spiritual practices, including witchcraft. This openness allowed for the re-emergence of ancient practices and beliefs, which resonated with those seeking a deeper connection to nature and a sense of personal empowerment.

Modern paganism and spiritual movements have been instrumental in furthering the acceptance of witchcraft. The growth of Neo-Pagan communities, with their public rituals and celebrations, has brought visibility and legitimacy to practices once marginalized. These communities often gather to celebrate the cycles of nature, marking events such as solstices and equinoxes with ceremonies that honor the earth and its energies. The emergence of Wicca, in particular, has played a crucial role in this cultural shift. Recognized as a religion in many parts of the world, Wicca emphasizes harmony with nature, the celebration of life, and personal responsibility. Its teachings have provided a structured framework for those seeking to explore witchcraft within a spiritual context, allowing for greater social acceptance and understanding.

The media and popular culture have also significantly contributed to the normalization of witchcraft. Film, television, and literature have evolved over the decades to present witches in a positive light, often as protagonists with complex personalities and motivations. Shows and movies have portrayed witches not just as villains or side characters but as heroes on their own journeys, exploring themes of empowerment, identity, and community. Books and stories have followed suit, weaving narratives that highlight the transformative power of magic and the strength found in embracing one's true self. These portrayals have helped to demystify witchcraft, making it more accessible and relatable to a wider audience.

Despite these advances, the acceptance of witchcraft continues to face challenges and debates. Misconceptions and stereotypes persist, often fueled by sensationalist media portrayals or misunderstandings of the practice. Some view witchcraft with suspicion, associating it with negative connotations or misunderstanding its spiritual and cultural significance. Additionally, practitioners of witchcraft may face social stigma or discrimination, particularly in areas where traditional or conservative beliefs dominate. These challenges underscore the importance of continued education and dialogue to foster understanding and acceptance.

As society becomes increasingly interconnected and diverse, the acceptance of witchcraft and other alternative spiritual practices will likely continue to grow. This chapter has explored the societal shifts and cultural changes that have contributed to this acceptance, highlighting the roles of Romanticism, the counterculture movement, modern paganism, and media. These influences have paved the way for a broader understanding of witchcraft, allowing it to be seen as a valid and enriching spiritual path. The journey from fear to acceptance reflects broader societal trends towards inclusivity and open-mindedness, setting the stage for the continued evolution of cultural narratives.

In the next chapter, you will discover how these changes have influenced modern interpretations of witchcraft and its role in contemporary society, as well as the ongoing efforts to preserve and celebrate the rich history and diverse practices associated with this enduring tradition.

CHAPTER 18
WITCHCRAFT AS A CULTURAL HERITAGE

WITCHCRAFT FESTIVALS: CELEBRATING HERITAGE

In the crisp autumn air of Salem, Massachusetts, where the leaves crunch underfoot and the sky hangs low with the promise of winter, the streets come alive with the whispers of the past. Here, in a town steeped in history, the month of October transforms into a spectacle of remembrance and celebration. Salem Haunted Happenings, a festival that stretches throughout the month, draws visitors from around the globe. They come not only to revel in the thrills of Halloween but also to engage with the echoes of a time when fear and superstition ruled the day. This festival turns the dark shadows of history into a vibrant tapestry of cultural heritage, inviting you to walk alongside the ghosts of the past and understand their stories.

Witchcraft festivals like Salem Haunted Happenings serve as powerful means of honoring and perpetuating witchcraft traditions. These events have grown into significant cultural celebrations that blend historical reflection with modern festivity. In Salem, the festival has become a cornerstone of the town's identity, contributing substantially to the local economy. According to recent reports, over 782 million dollars were injected into the region's economy last year, supporting thousands of jobs and generating significant tax revenue. Such economic benefits highlight the importance of these celebrations in sustaining local businesses and communities, reflecting a harmonious relationship between history and contemporary life.

Across the Atlantic, the Beltane Fire Festival in Edinburgh offers a different yet equally captivating celebration of witchcraft heritage. Held annually on Calton Hill, this festival resurrects the ancient Gaelic traditions that once marked the arrival of summer. A grand procession led by the May Queen and the Green Man, symbols of purity and rebirth, weaves through the festival, capturing the imagination of all who attend. While the festival draws on ancient practices, it also embraces modern interpretations, showcasing how cultural heritage can evolve and thrive in the present day. The vibrant displays of fire and physical theatre evoke a visceral connection to the past, inviting participants to leap over flames, just as their ancestors once did, in a symbolic act of purification and renewal.

These festivals offer diverse cultural expressions that

captivate both the heart and mind. Traditional dance and music performances transport you to another time, while artisan markets brim with crafts and wares that celebrate the creativity and skill of those who keep these traditions alive. Educational workshops provide an opportunity to delve deeper into the history and practices of witchcraft, offering insights into both ancient rituals and contemporary interpretations. Such events serve as vital educational platforms, dispelling myths and stereotypes by presenting witchcraft as a rich and multifaceted cultural heritage rather than a relic of superstition and fear.

The impact of witchcraft festivals extends beyond entertainment and education; they play a crucial role in strengthening community identity and pride. For the residents of Salem, Haunted Happenings is more than a tourist attraction; it is a celebration of resilience, a reminder of how the town has transformed its tragic past into a source of strength and unity. Similarly, the Beltane Fire Festival fosters a sense of belonging among its participants, creating a shared experience that transcends individual backgrounds and unites them in celebration of a common heritage. These festivals remind us of the power of shared history to forge connections and foster understanding.

Reflection Section: Engaging with Cultural Heritage

Consider attending a local festival or event that celebrates cultural heritage. Reflect on how participating in such events can deepen your understanding of history and its relevance to modern identity. Use this experience as an opportunity to explore your own cultural connections and consider how these shape your worldview.

The role of witchcraft festivals in dispelling stereotypes and educating the public is significant. By shining a light on the historical and cultural significance of witchcraft, these events challenge preconceived notions and encourage a more nuanced understanding of the past. They highlight the complexity and diversity of witchcraft traditions, offering a narrative that celebrates resilience and creativity rather than fear and persecution. Through these celebrations, we are invited to reexamine our relationship with history, recognizing that the stories of the past continue to shape and inform our present and future.

MUSEUMS AND EXHIBITIONS: PRESERVING WITCHCRAFT HISTORY

As you step inside a museum dedicated to the history of witchcraft, you find yourself surrounded by a world where artifacts whisper stories of the past. Museums play an invaluable role in preserving and interpreting the complex tapestry of witchcraft history, offering you a tangible connection to events and practices that once seemed shrouded in myth. Curators meticulously select and present artifacts that reveal the lives and beliefs of those who lived under the shadow of witchcraft accusations. Through carefully curated exhibits, these institutions bridge the gap between historical accounts and modern understanding, providing visitors with a nuanced view of witchcraft's legacy.

The Salem Witch Museum in Massachusetts stands as a poignant reminder of one of the most infamous periods of witchcraft hysteria. Here, you can explore the chilling events of 1692 through immersive exhibits that bring the trials to life. The museum offers a detailed narrative of the Salem witch trials, presenting artifacts such as courtroom sketches, personal letters, and legal documents that reveal the paranoia and fear that swept through the Puritan community. By examining these objects, you gain a deeper appreciation of the societal forces that fueled the witch hunts and the impact they had on the individuals involved. This museum not only educates visitors about the past but also encourages reflection on the lessons history has to offer.

In Germany, the Hexenbürgermeisterhaus in Lemgo provides another lens into the dark chapters of witchcraft history. This historic site, once the residence of the witch-hunting mayor Hermann Cothmann, now serves as a museum dedicated to the witch trials that plagued the region. Exhibits here include torture instruments, trial records, and personal belongings of the accused, each piece telling a story of suffering and injustice. As you wander through the rooms, you are confronted with the harsh realities faced by those accused of witchcraft, gaining insight into the cultural and religious contexts that allowed such persecution to occur. The Hexenbürgermeisterhaus preserves the memory of these events and serves as a somber reminder of the dangers of unchecked authority and the human capacity for cruelty.

Pendle Hill in Lancashire, England, offers yet another perspective on the history of witchcraft. This site is deeply entwined with the Pendle witch trials of 1612, where twelve individuals were accused of witchcraft and ten were executed. Though not a conventional museum, Pendle Hill offers you a chance to immerse yourself in the landscape that bore witness to these tragic events. Walking the pathways and exploring the surrounding countryside allows you to connect with the past in a profound way, imagining the lives of those who once called this place home. The story of the Pendle witches is further explored in local exhibitions, where artifacts and narratives shed light on the social and political dynamics that led to their persecution.

Museums and historical sites dedicated to witchcraft preserve the past and challenge contemporary perceptions. By presenting a multifaceted view of witchcraft history, these institutions encourage you to question stereotypes and consider the broader implications of witch hunts on modern society. They highlight the role of fear, superstition, and power in shaping historical events, prompting you to reflect on how these elements continue to influence our world today. Through their exhibits, museums foster a deeper understanding of the past, offering lessons in empathy, justice, and the importance of critical thinking.

As you engage with these histories, you are invited to consider the enduring impact of witchcraft beliefs and persecutions. Museums serve as gateways to understanding, connecting you with the stories of those who lived and suffered during these tumultuous times. They remind us that history is not just a collection of dates and events, but a tapestry of human experiences that continue to resonate in our lives. Through the preservation and interpretation of witchcraft history, museums offer a space for reflection and dialogue, encouraging us to learn from the past and shape a more informed future.

CHAPTER 19
EDUCATIONAL RESOURCES AND FURTHER EXPLORATION

I magine holding an old volume, its pages yellowed with age and filled with tales of witches and magic that have both haunted and fascinated humanity for centuries. The allure of witchcraft stretches beyond mere curiosity; it beckons us to explore the layers of history, culture, and belief that have shaped its narrative. As you delve deeper into the world of witchcraft, books become invaluable guides, offering insights into the lives and times of those who lived when the supernatural was as real as the rising sun. This chapter will guide you through a curated selection of readings that illuminate the complex tapestry of witchcraft history.

RECOMMENDED READING: BOOKS ON WITCHCRAFT HISTORY

To truly appreciate the historical context of witchcraft, foundational texts provide a solid grounding. "Witchcraft in Europe, 400-1700" by Alan Charles Kors and Edward Peters is a seminal work that delves into the evolution of witchcraft beliefs across the European continent, offering a comprehensive analysis of primary sources and scholarly interpretations. This book meticulously traces the changing perceptions and legal frameworks that defined witchcraft from the early medieval period through the dawn of the Enlightenment, making it an essential read for anyone interested in understanding the broader historical scope of witchcraft. Similarly, "The Witch-Hunt in Early Modern Europe" by Brian P. Levack examines the socio-political and religious factors that fueled witch hunts, providing a detailed exploration of the mechanisms of fear and control that led to one of history's most infamous periods.

Personal narratives and biographies offer a unique lens through which to view the human stories behind the witch trials. Stacy Schiff's "The Witches: Salem, 1692" paints a vivid picture of the Salem witch trials, blending meticulous research with narrative flair to bring to life the individuals caught in the crossfire of superstition and justice. Schiff's work captures the tension and paranoia that permeated Salem, offering readers a gripping account of this pivotal moment in American history. On a different note, Laurel Thatcher Ulrich's "Good Wives: Image and Reality in the

Lives of Women in Northern New England, 1650-1750" provides a nuanced exploration of women's roles and identities in early America, shedding light on how societal expectations and realities intersected with the witch trials.

Connecting historical events to modern themes, Kristen J. Sollee's "Witches, Sluts, Feminists: Conjuring the Sex Positive" reimagines the witch as a symbol of liberation and empowerment, exploring how historical narratives continue to influence contemporary gender politics. Sollee's work challenges readers to consider the witch's role in modern feminist discourse, offering a provocative and insightful perspective on how past perceptions shape present identities. Similarly, Silvia Federici's "Caliban and the Witch: Women, the Body and Primitive Accumulation" weaves together themes of capitalism, gender, and witchcraft, presenting a compelling argument about the socioeconomic forces that shaped witch hunts and their lasting impact on women's bodies and labor.

For those interested in exploring witchcraft beyond the Western lens, Angelique L'Amour's "African Wicca: The First African American Wicca Tradition" offers a fresh perspective on the intersection of African spirituality and Wiccan practices, highlighting the rich cultural diversity within modern witchcraft. Katherine Howe's "The Penguin Book of Witches" compiles historical documents and personal accounts from witch trials around the world, providing readers with a global perspective on witchcraft practices and their enduring legacy. These texts invite you to expand your understanding of witchcraft, encouraging a deeper appreciation of its cultural and historical significance.

DOCUMENTARIES AND FILMS: VISUAL JOURNEYS INTO WITCHCRAFT

Visual media is a powerful tool for exploring the complex world of witchcraft, offering a lens through which history, culture, and belief systems can be vividly brought to life. Documentaries like "The Burning Times," produced by the National Film Board of Canada, provide a haunting exploration of the European witch hunts. Through interviews and dramatizations, this film delves into the cultural and religious contexts that fueled centuries of persecution. It paints a poignant picture of fear and superstition, examining how societal dynamics turned suspicion into tragedy. Similarly, "Witches: A Century of Murder," a Channel 5 documentary, offers a gripping look at the witch trials in Britain. Narrated with historical precision, it uncovers the narratives of those accused and the societal mechanisms that led to their downfall, providing a chilling reminder of the destructive power of fear.

Films have long dramatized the harrowing events of witch trials, capturing their emotional and historical weight. "The Crucible," directed by Nicholas Hytner and based on Arthur Miller's acclaimed play, brings the Salem witch trials to life with intense emotion and stark realism. It explores the collision of personal vendettas and mass hysteria, revealing how unchecked fear can devastate a community. Another notable film, "Witchfinder General," directed by Michael Reeves, is set during the English Civil War and follows the grim exploits of a witch hunter. Its portrayal of the moral dilemmas and brutality inherent in witch hunts offers a sobering reflection on power and justice in turbulent times.

Modern witchcraft practices and communities are also well-documented in contemporary media. "American Mystic," directed by Alex Mar, provides an intimate look at the lives of modern spiritual practitioners, including a Pagan priestess, highlighting the personal and communal aspects of contemporary witchcraft. The film journeys into the heart of American spirituality, offering viewers an unvarnished glimpse into the daily lives and practices of those who find meaning in ancient traditions. The BBC documentary "A Very British Witchcraft" uncovers the origins and evolution of modern Wicca in Britain, tracing its roots back to the mid-20th century and exploring its impact on popular culture and spiritual identity.

Beyond history and modern practice, some films examine the broader cultural implications of witchcraft. "Häxan: Witchcraft Through the Ages," a 1922 silent film by Benjamin Christensen, is a groundbreaking work that blends documentary and dramatization to explore medieval witchcraft and its legacy. Its visually stunning sequences and innovative storytelling offer an early cinematic exploration of witchcraft's cultural impact. More recently, "The Witch: A New England Folktale," directed by Robert Eggers, immerses viewers in the atmospheric world of 17th-century Puritan New England. Through its meticulous attention to historical detail and psychological horror, it poses questions about faith, isolation, and the darkness within human nature.

ENGAGING WITH WITCHCRAFT IN ACADEMIA

Witchcraft, as a subject of academic inquiry, opens doors to a myriad of perspectives, each adding depth to our understanding of its role in human history. Through the lens of anthropology, scholars examine cultural practices surrounding witchcraft, seeking to understand how these beliefs reflect social structures and values. Anthropologists often immerse themselves in communities, observing rituals and gathering oral histories that shed light on how witchcraft has been used to enforce social norms or challenge authority. This approach not only reveals the diversity of witchcraft practices across cultures but also highlights common themes that resonate universally, such as the use of magic for protection or empowerment.

Historical analysis offers another rich avenue for exploring witchcraft. By delving into legal proceedings and trial records, historians unravel the complex interplay of fear, power, and justice that characterized witch hunts. This method allows for a nuanced understanding of how legal systems evolved in response to societal pressures, illustrating the balance between reason and superstition. These studies also reveal the socio-political contexts that made witch trials possible, offering lessons on the consequences of unchecked authority and mass hysteria. At the intersection of history and the arts, witchcraft's influence on literature and art studies cannot be overstated. Literary scholars dissect texts from various periods to explore how witches have been portrayed, from Shakespeare's enigmatic hags to the empowered figures in modern narratives. Art historians, similarly, examine visual representations of witches, tracing how these images have reflected and shaped societal attitudes over time.

For those eager to pursue formal study, a variety of academic programs focus on witchcraft history. Institutions like the University of Exeter offer specialized courses that examine magic and witchcraft through historical and cultural lenses. These courses provide students with the tools to critically engage with primary sources and develop their own interpretations. Online platforms like Coursera and edX also offer courses, making these topics accessible to a global audience. These programs often incorporate interdisciplinary approaches, encouraging students to explore witchcraft from multiple perspectives and fostering a deeper understanding of its complexities.

Engagement doesn't stop at the classroom door. Conferences and symposiums provide dynamic forums for discussion and discovery. Events like the International Conference on Witchcraft Studies and the Annual Symposium on Medieval and Renaissance Studies bring together scholars from around the world to share their latest research and insights. These gatherings offer participants the opportunity to engage with leading experts, exchange ideas, and explore new avenues of inquiry. For aspiring researchers, these events can also provide valuable networking opportunities, opening doors to collaboration and mentorship.

For those interested in contributing to the academic conversation, numerous opportunities exist for research and publication. Accessing archives and primary sources is often the first step; university libraries and online databases can be treasure troves of historical documents and artifacts. Aspiring scholars may consider submitting their work to journals specializing in witchcraft studies, where they can reach an audience of peers and experts eager for fresh perspectives.

CHAPTER 20

CONTEMPORARY WITCHCRAFT PRACTICES

NEO-PAGANISM: A REVIVAL OF ANCIENT PRACTICES

In a world increasingly dominated by technology and urban sprawl, a movement quietly flourishes, inviting you to step away from the hum of machines and into the whispering embrace of the natural world. Neo-Paganism, a revival of ancient spiritual practices, offers a sanctuary for those seeking to reconnect with the rhythms of the earth. Emerging in the 20th century as a response to industrialization, Neo-Paganism weaves together threads of history, spirituality, and a yearning for harmony with nature. Amidst the clamor of modern life, this movement reminds us of our deep-seated connection to the earth and its cycles, encouraging a return to simpler, more mindful ways of being.

The roots of Neo-Paganism stretch back to the early

20th century, inspired by the burgeoning interest in occultism and esoteric traditions. Figures like Gerald Gardner played a pivotal role in bringing these ancient practices into the modern world. Gardner, often regarded as the father of modern Wicca, crafted a spiritual framework that blended elements of ceremonial magic, Freemasonry, and folklore. His writings, such as "Witchcraft Today," laid the foundation for Wicca, a tradition that has now spread worldwide. Alongside Gardner, Doreen Valiente, a key figure in the development of Wicca, enriched the movement with her poetic invocations and emphasis on natural magic. Valiente's contributions helped shape the rituals and beliefs that define Neo-Paganism today.

As industrialization reshaped landscapes and lifestyles, Neo-Paganism offered a spiritual counterbalance, emphasizing a return to nature. The environmental movement, gaining momentum in the latter half of the 20th century, further influenced Neo-Pagan practices, aligning them with ecological consciousness. This alignment is evident in the reverence for the earth as a sacred entity and the celebration of natural cycles, such as the Wheel of the Year. This calendar of festivals marks the changing seasons, honoring the solstices and equinoxes with rituals that celebrate life's cyclical nature. These festivities, known as Sabbats, are times of reflection and renewal, inviting you to participate in the timeless dance of the seasons.

Central to Neo-Paganism is the belief in polytheism and the veneration of ancient deities. These spiritual practices often draw on a pantheon of gods and goddesses from various mythologies, each representing different aspects of life and the natural world. This polytheistic approach allows for a rich tapestry of beliefs and rituals, fostering a deep connection to the divine in its many forms. The practices are as diverse as the deities themselves, reflecting the individual paths of practitioners who may choose to honor specific gods or integrate elements from different traditions.

Neo-Paganism is not a monolith but a diverse tapestry of traditions and paths. Within this movement, you will find Wiccans, who often work in covens and follow a structured set of rituals and beliefs, and Druids, who are drawn to the wisdom of ancient Celtic practices. Heathenry, which revives Norse and Germanic traditions, offers another path, focusing on ancestral heritage and community bonds. Some Neo-Pagans prefer solitary practice, finding personal meaning and spiritual growth outside of formal groups. This diversity reflects a core tenet of Neo-Paganism: the freedom to explore and define one's spiritual journey.

The societal and cultural impact of Neo-Paganism is profound, influencing modern spirituality and cultural identity. By promoting environmental awareness, Neo-Paganism encourages a profound respect for nature and a commitment to ecological sustainability. This awareness is reflected in the growing emphasis on living in harmony with the earth, adopting practices that honor and preserve its resources. The movement's influence extends beyond spirituality, weaving into contemporary art and literature. Artists and writers draw inspiration from Neo-Pagan themes, exploring ideas of transformation, interconnectedness, and the sacredness of the natural world. Through these expressions, Neo-Paganism continues to shape cultural narratives, offering an alternative vision of spirituality that resonates with the complexities and challenges of modern life.

CONTEMPORARY WITCHES: PRACTICES AND BELIEFS

In today's world, the figure of the witch is as diverse and multifaceted as the cultures and traditions that influence modern witchcraft. Contemporary witches often embrace eclecticism, a practice that involves drawing from a variety of spiritual traditions to create a unique and personalized path. This approach allows practitioners to incorporate elements from different belief systems, such as Eastern philosophies, indigenous rituals, and Western esoteric traditions, into their practices. This blending of traditions reflects a larger trend toward individualization in spirituality, where personal experience and intuition guide the creation of one's spiritual path. The flexibility of eclecticism suits the dynamic nature of contemporary society, allowing witches to adapt and evolve their practices in response to new influences and insights.

Technology and social media have dramatically transformed how modern witches share their practices and build communities. Platforms like Instagram, TikTok, and online forums provide spaces for witches to connect, share knowledge, and support one another. These digital communities offer a sense of belonging and facilitate the exchange of ideas, rituals, and experiences across geographic and cultural boundaries. Social media also plays a crucial role in normalizing witchcraft, as practitioners share their stories and demystify their practices for a broader audience. However, while the internet has expanded access to information, it also presents challenges, such as the spread of misinformation and the commodification of spiritual practices. Despite these challenges, the online presence of witchcraft continues to grow, enriching the lives of practitioners and fostering a global community.

In contemporary witchcraft, personal spirituality and individual pathfinding are emphasized, encouraging witches to explore their beliefs and practices independently. This focus on personal empowerment resonates with individuals seeking a spiritual path that aligns with their values and experiences. Witches often engage in self-reflection and experimentation, drawing on various sources of inspiration to develop a practice that feels authentic and meaningful. This individualistic approach allows for a wide range of expressions within the witchcraft community, where practitioners are free to explore their spirituality without the constraints of dogma or rigid structures.

Tools and symbols play a significant role in modern witchcraft, serving as conduits for spiritual energy and intention. Crystals, tarot cards, and pendulums are popular tools used in divination, each offering unique insights and guidance. Crystals are believed to possess specific energetic properties that can enhance healing, protection, or manifestation efforts. Tarot cards provide a visual language for exploring the subconscious and gaining clarity on life's challenges. Pendulums, often used for dowsing, offer a simple yet powerful method for accessing intuitive insights. The pentacle, a five-pointed star within a circle, is a sacred symbol in witchcraft, representing the elements, spirit, and the interconnectedness of all things. These tools and symbols are integral to modern witchcraft, allowing practitioners to deepen their connection to the spiritual realm and express their intentions with clarity and focus.

Contemporary witches are increasingly engaging with social and political issues, using their practices as a form of activism and empowerment. Many witches participate in social justice movements, advocating for equality, environmental sustainability, and human rights. Witchcraft serves as a powerful tool for protest, with rituals and spells used to channel energy toward positive change and resistance against oppression. This activism is often rooted in the belief that personal transformation can lead to broader societal change, reflecting the interconnectedness of all beings. Through their engagement with social and political issues, witches demonstrate the relevance of their practices in addressing the challenges of the modern world.

Despite the growing acceptance of witchcraft, practitioners still face challenges and misconceptions. Mainstream media often portrays witchcraft in sensationalized or inaccurate ways, perpetuating stereotypes and misunderstandings. These portrayals can lead to prejudice and discrimination, affecting how witches are perceived by the broader public. To combat these misconceptions, many witches engage in public outreach and community events, seeking to educate others about the true nature of their practices. By sharing their stories and experiences, witches aim to dispel myths and promote a deeper understanding of witchcraft as a legitimate and meaningful spiritual path. Through these efforts, they strive to create a more inclusive and accepting society, where diverse spiritual traditions are respected and celebrated.

CHAPTER 21
THE FUTURE OF WITCHCRAFT STUDIES

DIGITAL WITCHCRAFT: THE INTERNET AND WITCHCRAFT COMMUNITIES

I n the quiet corners of the digital world, a new kind of magic is brewing. Witchcraft, long shrouded in mystery and practiced in secluded spaces, is now finding a vibrant home on the internet. This shift is not merely about accessibility; it represents a profound transformation in how practitioners connect, share, and evolve their craft. Digital platforms have become the modern-day covens where witches from around the globe gather, transcending geographical boundaries and cultural barriers. Within this virtual realm, the exchange of ideas and experiences flourishes, fostering a sense of community that is both inclusive and dynamic.

The internet plays a crucial role in connecting and expanding witch communities. It provides a space where individuals can come together, share practices, and offer support. Online forums and discussion groups serve as digital hearths where you can exchange knowledge and insights. Websites and blogs dedicated to witchcraft abound, offering a wealth of educational resources that cover everything from ancient rituals to modern adaptations. These platforms are invaluable for both novice witches seeking guidance and seasoned practitioners looking to expand their horizons. They offer a sense of belonging and a chance to engage with a global network of like-minded individuals, enriching the practice of witchcraft in ways previously unimaginable.

Social media has further amplified the visibility and perception of witchcraft. Platforms like Instagram and TikTok have transformed the way witches present themselves and their practices. On these platforms, popular witch influencers shape trends and set the tone for contemporary witchcraft. They share rituals, spells, and personal experiences, demystifying the practice and making it more accessible to newcomers. Hashtags connect practitioners, facilitating the discovery of new content and fostering a sense of community. These digital spaces not only showcase the diversity within the witchcraft community but also highlight its adaptability and resilience in the face of modern challenges. However, this visibility comes with its own set of challenges.

The rise of digital witchcraft presents both opportunities and pitfalls. On one hand, the internet allows for unprecedented global collaboration and cultural exchange, enabling witches to learn from diverse traditions and incorporate them into their practices. On the other hand, the digital realm is rife with misinformation and the commodification of witchcraft. The commercialization of spiritual practices can dilute their meaning and authenticity, turning deeply personal rituals into marketable products. This commodification can lead to a superficial understanding of witchcraft, where aesthetics overshadow substance. Practitioners must navigate this landscape carefully, discerning genuine wisdom from the noise of consumerism. Despite these challenges, the potential for growth and innovation within digital witchcraft communities remains vast.

Digital tools are increasingly integrated into modern witchcraft practices, offering new ways to engage with the craft. Apps dedicated to astrology and lunar phases help you attune to celestial rhythms, while virtual reality creates immersive ritual spaces that transcend physical limitations. Online tarot readings and digital spellcasting tools provide convenience and accessibility, allowing you to practice anywhere, at any time. These technologies can enhance traditional practices, offering new dimensions and perspectives. However, they also require careful consideration, ensuring that the core principles of witchcraft—intent, connection, and authenticity—are not lost in the digital translation.

FUTURE RESEARCH DIRECTIONS IN WITCHCRAFT STUDIES

In the ever-evolving landscape of witchcraft studies, new avenues of inquiry are continually emerging, each offering fresh perspectives and insights. One burgeoning area of interest lies at the intersection of witchcraft and environmental studies. Scholars are increasingly exploring how traditional practices and beliefs can inform and enhance our understanding of ecological stewardship. This line of inquiry considers how the reverence for nature inherent in many witchcraft traditions can contribute to contemporary environmental ethics. It examines rituals and beliefs that emphasize harmony with the earth, seeking ways to integrate these time-honored practices into modern sustainability efforts. Such research enriches our understanding of witchcraft and highlights its potential role in addressing today's environmental challenges.

Another promising area is the role of witchcraft in queer and gender studies. The historical association of witches with marginalized groups makes this an intriguing subject for scholars examining issues of identity and power. Researchers are delving into how witchcraft has been both a tool of oppression and a means of resistance for queer communities. They explore how modern witches are reclaiming these identities, using the symbol of the witch as a form of empowerment and subversion. This research shines a light on the dynamic interplay between tradition and modern identity, offering a deeper understanding of how witchcraft continues to shape and be shaped by issues of gender and sexuality today.

The examination of witchcraft in non-traditional cultural contexts also presents new opportunities for scholarly exploration. As globalization influences cultural exchange, researchers are interested in how witchcraft is practiced and perceived across different societies. This includes studying indigenous traditions that have remained largely undocumented or misunderstood. By examining these practices, scholars can uncover rich cultural narratives that challenge conventional Western perspectives on witchcraft. This research is crucial for preserving diverse cultural heritages and for fostering a more inclusive understanding of witchcraft's role in the world.

Interdisciplinary approaches are proving invaluable in advancing witchcraft studies. Collaboration between historians, anthropologists, and psychologists enriches our understanding by bringing together diverse methodologies and insights. Historians provide context and continuity, anthropologists offer cultural and societal perspectives, while psychologists explore the cognitive and emotional dimensions of belief and practice. The integration of digital humanities tools further enhances this research, allowing for sophisticated analysis of historical texts. These tools enable scholars to uncover patterns and connections that might otherwise remain hidden, making it possible to explore the rich tapestry of witchcraft's historical and cultural evolution with greater depth and precision.

Preserving oral histories and indigenous practices is another critical aspect of contemporary witchcraft research. In many communities, oral traditions serve as the primary means of transmitting knowledge and ensuring cultural continuity. Efforts to record and preserve these stories are essential, not only for safeguarding cultural heritage but also for enriching our understanding of witchcraft's diverse expressions. This research into the impact of globalization on indigenous practices helps to highlight both the vulnerabilities and the resilience of these traditions. By documenting the experiences of living practitioners, scholars can capture a vibrant and dynamic picture of witchcraft, one that honors the past while embracing the future.

However, conducting research in this field presents unique challenges and ethical considerations. Scholars must navigate the delicate balance between academic inquiry and respect for practitioners' beliefs. This requires sensitivity and a commitment to ethical standards, ensuring that research does not exploit or misrepresent the communities it seeks to understand. Cultural sensitivity is paramount, as is the avoidance of appropriation, which can often occur when external parties engage with indigenous and marginalized traditions. Researchers must also be mindful of the power dynamics at play, striving to ensure that their work empowers and amplifies the voices of those they study, rather than overshadowing them.

～

AFTERWORD

As we close this journey through the rich tapestry of witchcraft's history, let us revisit the intriguing path we have traveled together. From the ancient rituals of Mesopotamia and Egypt to the mystical practices of the Celts and Druids, witchcraft has been interwoven with humanity's cultural and religious fabric. We've explored classical antiquity, where figures like Hecate and Circe blurred the lines between myth and reality, setting the stage for centuries of magical interpretation. The medieval period, with its intense witch hunts and fear-driven perse-cutions, showed us how societal anxieties can manifest as witchcraft accusations, impacting countless lives across Europe.

Throughout these historical explorations, several themes have emerged, offering profound insights into the enduring legacy of witchcraft. Gender and power dynamics have been central to the narrative, revealing how societal structures often targeted women, using witchcraft as a tool of control. The role of fear and superstition has underscored how deeply ingrained beliefs can shape actions and policies, sometimes to devastating effect. Over the centuries, perceptions of witchcraft have transformed from feared practices to symbols of empowerment and resistance, reflecting broader societal changes.

Our journey didn't stop at Western narratives. We ventured into the global landscape, uncovering the diverse expressions of witchcraft across continents. From the spiritual traditions of Africa and Indigenous North American cultures to the mystical practices in Asia and the enduring influences in Latin America, witchcraft emerged as a multifaceted phenomenon. Each culture offered unique perspectives, enriching our understanding and challenging us to see witchcraft as a complex, culturally significant element worldwide.

In modern times, the echoes of historical witchcraft resonate in contemporary society. Neo-Paganism and feminist movements have reclaimed and redefined the witch as a figure of strength and autonomy. Pop culture has embraced these narratives, presenting witches as complex characters who captivate and inspire. These modern interpretations honor the past and offer fresh insights into our cultural identity today.

Witchcraft, as we have seen, is not merely a relic of the past but a dynamic and enduring legacy. It continues to shape societal norms, influence cultural identities, and inspire modern spirituality. By challenging stereotypes and inviting deeper reflection, this book aims to provide a nuanced perspective on witchcraft's historical and cultural significance.

I encourage you to delve deeper into this fascinating subject. The recommended resources offer pathways for further exploration, whether through books, documentaries, or academic courses. Engage with local cultural events or visit museums to witness witchcraft's history firsthand. Participate in community discussions to expand your understanding and appreciation of this rich heritage.

My motivation for writing this book stems from a desire to dispel myths and promote understanding. Witchcraft holds a vital place in our global cultural tapestry, deserving recognition and respect. I invite you to join me in fostering a more informed dialogue about witchcraft, embracing its complexities and celebrating its global significance. Together, we can continue to explore and appreciate witchcraft as a source of historical insight and cultural inspiration.

If you enjoyed this book, please consider leaving a review. Your feedback helps support independent publishers and makes a big difference in spreading the word to other readers.

BIBLIOGRAPHY

Ašipu. (n.d.). In *Wikipedia*. Retrieved October 26, 2024, from https://en. wikipedia.org/wiki/A%C5%A1ipu#:~:text=A%C5%A1ipu%20direct-ed%20medical%20treatment%20at,the%20remedies%20indicat-ed%20by%20diagnosis.

Book of the Dead: Spells. (n.d.). *Passport to the Egyptian Afterlife*. Retrieved October 26, 2024, from https://book-of-the-dead.fitzmuseum.cam. ac.uk/explore/book-of-the-dead/spells

Under the Spell of the Druids. (n.d.). *History Today*. Retrieved October 26, 2024, from https://www.historytoday.com/miscellanies/under-spell-druids

Sacred Sites & Rituals in the Ancient Celtic Religion. (n.d.). *World History Encyclopedia*. Retrieved October 26, 2024, from https://www.world history.org/article/1710/sacred-sites--rituals-in-the-ancient-celtic-religi/

HECATE (Hekate) - Greek Goddess of Witchcraft, Magic & ... (n.d.). *Theoi Greek Mythology*. Retrieved October 26, 2024, from https://www. theoi.com/Khthonios/Hekate.html

Curse Tablets and Our Understanding of the Ancient World. (n.d.). *Ekklesia Magazine*. Retrieved October 26, 2024, from https://ekklesia mag.wordpress.com/curse-tablets-and-our-understanding-of-the-ancient-world/

The Interdiction of Magic in Roman Law. (n.d.). *JSTOR*. Retrieved October 26, 2024, from https://www.jstor.org/stable/ 283219#:~:text=In%20Roman%20law%20the%20antisocial,ritu-al%20murder)%2C%20philters%2C%20.

Courtroom Drama: Apuleius' Apologia. (n.d.). In *Oxford Academic*. Retrieved October 26, 2024, from https://academic.oup.com/book/ 8066/chapter/153463079

From Paganism to Christianity. (n.d.). *Harvard University*. Retrieved October 26, 2024, from https://chs.harvard.edu/chapter/2-from-paganism-to-christianity/

BIBLIOGRAPHY

Magic | Early and Medieval Christian Heresy. (n.d.). *UO Blogs*. Retrieved October 26, 2024, from https://blogs.uoregon.edu/rel424s15drreis/magic/

Elvira (Iliberri). (n.d.). *Legal History Sources*. Retrieved October 26, 2024, from http://legalhistorysources.com/Canon%20Law/ElviraCanons.htm

Martyr of the Week: Priscillian of Ávila. (2014, March 7). *Fascinating Mystery*. Retrieved October 26, 2024, from https://fascinatingmystery.wordpress.com/2014/03/07/martyr-of-the-week-priscillian-of-avila/

How the Malleus Maleficarum Fueled the Witch Trial Craze. (2024, October). *Ars Technica*. Retrieved October 26, 2024, from https://arstechnica.com/science/2024/10/how-the-malleus-maleficarum-fueled-the-witch-trial-craze/

Witch Hunts: From Salem to Guantanamo Bay. (n.d.). *JSTOR*. Retrieved October 26, 2024, from https://www.jstor.org/stable/j.ctt819pr#:~:text=These%20were%20the%20great%20witch,just%20a%20few%20miles%20away.

The Eichstätt Witch-Hunts. (n.d.). *H-Net Reviews*. Retrieved October 26, 2024, from https://www.h-net.org/reviews/showrev.php?id=14719

Witchcraft - Medieval Studies. (n.d.). *Oxford Bibliographies*. Retrieved October 26, 2024, from https://www.oxfordbibliographies.com/abstract/document/obo-9780195396584/obo-9780195396584-0190.xml

Misogyny: The Driving Force of the Great European Witch Hunts. (2021, October 24). *Retrospect Journal*. Retrieved October 26, 2024, from https://retrospectjournal.com/2021/10/24/misogyny-the-driving-force-of-the-great-european-witch-hunts-from-the-fifteenth-to-seventeenth-centuries/

Witchcraft Accusations Were an 'Occupational Hazard' for Women. (n.d.). *University of Cambridge*. Retrieved October 26, 2024, from https://www.cam.ac.uk/stories/witchcraft-work-women

Anne Boleyn and the Charge of Witchcraft: A Guest Post by Claire Ridgway. (n.d.). *Susan Higginbotham*. Retrieved October 26, 2024, from https://www.susanhigginbotham.com/posts/anne-boleyn-and-the-charge-of-witchcraft-a-guest-post-by-claire-ridgway/#:~:text=She%20was%20charged%20with%20treason-able,she%20was%20charged%20with%20it.

Witches as Metaphors: Francisco Goya's Image of the Witch. (n.d.). *Salem Witch Museum.* Retrieved October 26, 2024, from https://salemwitchmuseum.com/2020/05/21/witches-as-metaphors-fran cisco-goyas-image-of-the-witch/

Fact or Fiction: The Role of Witchcraft and Juju in Africa. (n.d.). *Medium.* Retrieved October 26, 2024, from https://medium.com/@mcaddow/fact-or-fiction-the-role-of-witchcraft-and-juju-in-africa-39ecc220faef

Witchcraft in Africa: Political Power and Spiritual Insecurity. (n.d.). *Oxford Research Encyclopedia of African History.* Retrieved October 26, 2024, from https://oxfordre.com/africanhistory/display/10.1093/acre fore/9780190277734.001.0001/acrefore-9780190277734-e-441?d=% 2F10.1093%2Facrefore%2F9780190277734.001.0001%2Facrefore-9780190277734-e-441&p=emailAkD1pC1FXeUiM

Navajo Skinwalkers – Witches of the Southwest. (n.d.). *Legends of America.* Retrieved October 26, 2024, from https://www.legendso famerica.com/navajo-skinwalkers/

North American Shamanism. (n.d.). *Encyclopedia.com.* Retrieved October 26, 2024, from https://www.encyclopedia.com/environment/encyclo pedias-almanacs-transcripts-and-maps/shamanism-north-ameri can-shamanism

Witchcraft, Economy and Society in the Forest of Pendle. (n.d.). *Research-Gate.* Retrieved October 26, 2024, from https://www.researchgate.net/publication/300204531_Witchcraft_economy_and_society_in_the_forest_of_Pendle

Spectral Evidence and the Salem Witch Trials. (n.d.). *ThoughtCo.* Retrieved October 26, 2024, from https://www.thoughtco.com/what-is-spectral-evidence-3528204

King James I and the Witch Hunts of Scotland. (n.d.). *National Geographic.* Retrieved October 26, 2024, from https://www.national geographic.com/history/history-magazine/article/scotland-witch-hunts

The Puritan Religion and How it Influenced the Salem Witch Trials. (n.d.). *UK Essays.* Retrieved October 26, 2024, from https://www.

ukessays.com/essays/history/influence-of-the-puritan-religion-on-the-salem-witch-trials.php

Magic and Law at the Border: The Early Medieval Leges. (n.d.). *OAJournals*. Retrieved October 26, 2024, from https://oajournals.fupress.net/index.php/bsfm-lea/article/download/14936/13676

Constitutio Criminalis Carolina (1532) [Excerpts]. (n.d.). Retrieved October 26, 2024, from https://pages.uoregon.edu/dluebke/Witches442/ConstitutioCriminalis.html

The Possession at Loudun, de Certeau, Smith. (n.d.). *University of Chicago Press*. Retrieved October 26, 2024, from https://press.uchicago.edu/ucp/books/book/chicago/P/bo3626714.html

Witchcraft & the Law in Early Modern Europe & USA: England. (n.d.). *Bodleian Libraries*. Retrieved October 26, 2024, from https://libguides.bodleian.ox.ac.uk/law-witch/england

The Inquisitorial System and its Impact on the Witch-Hunts. (n.d.). *Chronos*. Retrieved October 26, 2024, from https://surface.syr.edu/cgi/viewcontent.cgi?article=1079&context=chronos#:~: